Suffolk
MURDERS

MARK MOWER

The
History
Press

First published 2011

Reprinted 2012, 2013

The History Press
The Mill, Brimscombe Port
Stroud, Gloucestershire, GL5 2QG
www.thehistorypress.co.uk

British Library Cataloguing in Publication Data.
A catalogue record for this book is available from the British Library.

ISBN 978 0 7524 4905 0

Typesetting and origination by The History Press
Printed and bound in Great Britain by
Marston Book Services Limited, Oxfordshire

CONTENTS

ACKNOWLEDGEMENTS

Crime writing is a curious and singular profession which, like many of the misdemeanours it seeks to document, is usually perpetrated alone and behind closed doors. That said, a large number of people have helped me in the research and production of this book and for their assistance and encouragement I am extremely indebted.

As ever, there were certain individuals who provided invaluable assistance – sometimes beyond the call of duty – to whom I would like to express my particular gratitude: Brian Dyes of the Ipswich Transport Museum, for access to information on Frederick Storey and the tramway system of Ipswich; Terry Lynes of the Lowestoft Heritage Workshop Centre for many of the older photographs and for crucial information on the Junction Passage Murder; Charles Sale of the Gravestone Photographic Resource (www.gravestonephotos.com) for the image of William Napthen's grave; Lisa Spurrier, archivist with the Berkshire Record Office, for help with material on Frederick Page contained in the archives for Broadmoor Hospital; Richard Moles for assisting with some of the background research on John Mickleburgh; Clare Everitt, Picture Norfolk Administrator, for providing me with access to some of the unique images contained in Norfolk County Council's online database (www.picture. norfolk.gov.uk); Jonathan Plunkett, for use of some of the marvellous photographs of old Norwich taken by his father in the early part of the twentieth century (www.georgeplunkett.co.uk); Tony Morley, for taking a picture of Kessingland Church in the coldest spell of the 2010 winter;

Venita Paul, Senior Picture Researcher of the Wellcome Library, for access to its image archive; Mike Fordham, Curator of Halesworth Museum, for the picture of Ebenezer Tye's grave; Anne Cronin of the White Horse Inn in Stoke Ash, for the early picture of the pub (www.whitehorse-suffolk. co.uk); and staff of the Suffolk Record Offices in Lowestoft, Ipswich and Bury St Edmunds, for their vital knowledge and guidance.

Finally, I would like to thank my family for putting up with me during the many months I have been locked away in my study, tapping away at a computer keyboard, completely oblivious to the outside world. The love and support of my wife Jacqueline and daughter Rosie makes it all worthwhile.

All of the photographs and illustrations that appear in the book are from my own camera or collection unless otherwise acknowledged.

INTRODUCTION

The county of Suffolk stretches from the chalky downlands of Newmarket in the west to Britain's easternmost point – Lowestoft – on the coast. North to south, the landscape takes in the lowland forests and sandy brecklands of Brandon to the gently undulating valleys and picturesque beauty that is 'Constable Country'. From its agricultural and maritime roots, Suffolk has remained a county of endearing contrasts: splendidly secluded, yet reassuringly inviting; large and diverse, yet intimately familiar; immediately appealing, yet bewitching for its hidden treasures.

Much is often made about the county's agricultural heritage and the impact of this on the social, economic and environmental conditions of its many towns and villages. In 1841, over 40 per cent of the local population was employed in the cultivation of land, compared to an already declining 20 per cent in the rest of England and Wales. And while this proportion would decline in the 100 years that followed, Suffolk, like other parts of East Anglia, would retain a disproportionate share of the nation's agricultural workforce.

While the county's agricultural heritage added much colour to the particular customs and practices of the local population, it also created a stark backdrop to the lives of many ordinary people. Rural poverty manifested itself all too often in inadequate housing, poor sanitation and appalling working conditions and the seasonal, unskilled and weather-dependent nature of much agricultural work helped to keep wages low. This in turn led to poor health, starvation, disease, alcoholism and early death. Crucially, this poverty also led to crime, and the social conditions and attitudes created by the insular and rural nature of the county often gave rise to particular types of offences – from highway robbery, smuggling and poaching, to incidents of appalling child cruelty. Some crimes reflected the narrow-mindedness shown to outsiders and those with mental health problems, which could often prompt suicide or murder. Others simply reflected the criminal preoccupations of their time – from body-snatching to arsenical poisoning.

Despite this, Suffolk has always been a comparatively tranquil and safe place to live. For generations it has maintained a reputation as a sleepy rural backwater when considered against other more densely populated counties. But the nature of rural life has at times produced its own transgressions and tragedies – the deaths and murders which have resulted from bigotry, jealousy, fear and crime.

It was Sherlock Holmes, Arthur Conan Doyle's fictional detective mastermind, who opined:

> It is my belief, Watson, founded upon my experience, that the lowest and vilest alleys in London do not present a more dreadful record of sin than does the smiling and beautiful countryside ... But look at these lonely houses, each in its own fields, filled for the most part with poor ignorant folk who know little of the law. Think of the deeds of hellish cruelty, the hidden wickedness which may go on, year in, year out, in such places, and none the wiser. (The Copper Beeches)

A look at some of the more notorious murder cases from Suffolk's past lends some credence to the great detective's observations. For the disarming allure of its rural idyll has occasionally been tarnished by some of the most despicable of human acts. Two of the most infamous and well-documented cases serve to illustrate this.

The first occurred in Peasenhall, a picture-postcard village in mid-Suffolk which has retained the look of a nineteenth-century hamlet and still has its original grocery store – Emmett's has been trading from the site since 1840 and continues to provide some of the finest smoked ham and bacon in the east of England. Despite its harmonious setting, the village is remembered most often as the scene of an intriguing murder mystery in 1902, when servant girl Rose Annie Harsent had her throat cut and died in the home of her employer. William Gardiner, a local choirmaster and Sunday school teacher, was tried for the crime, although two separate juries failed to find him guilty. The real perpetrator of the Peasenhall Murder remains unknown.

Providence House, the scene of the Peasenhall Murder. The attic bedroom of Rose Annie Harsent can be seen at the top of the house.

The second took place in the south-west of the county, in the equally appealing village of Polstead which sits on the River Box. The 'Murder in the Red Barn' has passed into legend, although the tale of Maria Marten's death was real enough. She was the young daughter of a local mole catcher, who set off from her family home on 18 May 1827 never to be seen again. Marten had agreed to meet her twenty-four-year-old lover, William Corder, in order to marry. He owned the land on which their chosen meeting place – the Red Barn – was situated. In April 1828, her dead body was discovered in a shallow grave within the barn and Corder was arrested and brought to trial. Having been found guilty of murder he was hanged at Bury St Edmunds later that year. The sordid nature of the crime continues to fascinate today.

A Correct View of the Red Barn. Polstead Barn was destroyed by fire some years since

Early engravings depicting scenes from the Murder in the Red Barn.

Murders like those of Maria Marten and Rose Harsent became a focus for public gossip, speculation and wider social debate within Suffolk. They also created an insatiable demand for printed media. The publication of execution broadsheets flourished and nineteenth- and early twentieth-century newspapers covered significant murders in all their gory details. But it would be wrong to assume that this reflected only a prurient fascination with crime and death. Many within the county were willing to challenge the inhumanity of capital punishment and large-scale petitions for the reprieve of condemned prisoners were not uncommon (as Chapter 2 illustrates). Others campaigned for improvements in the social and economic conditions which gave rise to so much of the crime which blighted their communities.

The ability of the authorities to detect, investigate and prosecute criminals for their misdemeanours has a long history in Suffolk as elsewhere. In the Anglo-Saxon period, law and order was a community responsibility, with every man having the power to arrest those breaking the law and to take them before a court. Failure to act in this capacity was, in itself, a crime. For law-breaking on a larger scale, the sheriff of the county could co-opt a group of local men – known as a *posse comitatus* – to protect towns and villages and bring criminal gangs to justice.

Nationally, it was Henry II who first began to reorganise the criminal justice system in ways that we would recognise today. From 1154, using his talented chancellor Thomas Becket, Henry established prisons for those awaiting trial and courts to try those suspected of wrongdoing. These 'assizes' gave fast and clear verdicts and extended royal control. In granting manorial privileges, Henry also often allowed for the erection of gallows and tumbrill – an authority to retain a ducking-chair for the administration of justice. This was used primarily for the punishment of scolds and brawling women. Surviving examples of these insidious instruments of torture can still be found across the county.

The reign of Richard I brought further changes, not least of which was the introduction from 1195 of a system of lay magistrates to preserve the peace in unruly areas. Specially chosen knights were responsible to the King for ensuring that the law was upheld. In effect, they preserved the 'King's Peace'. From 1361, those undertaking this role became known as Justices of the Peace (JPs) and retained the power to bind over unruly persons 'to be of good behaviour'. Since that time, JPs have continued to carry out the greater part of the judicial work undertaken in England and Wales on behalf of the sovereign. The Act of 1361 also provided that JPs should meet to conduct local business four times a year – the origin of the 'Quarter Sessions' – which continued until replaced by Crown Courts in January 1972.

"DUCKING CHAIR
CHRISTCHURCH MANSION,
IPSWICH.

The manorial privileges granted by King Henry II from 1154 often allowed for the erection of gallows and tumbril – an authority to retain a ducking-chair for the administration of justice. The picture shows a surviving Suffolk example of this insidious instrument of torture.

JPs were also responsible for maintaining the earliest system of policing in the country. In 1576, they were required to build 'houses of correction' in which rogues and vagabonds could be detained. These were apprehended by parish constables who were unpaid parishioners conscripted for service annually. With no uniforms or warrant cards at this time, each individual carried only a decorated truncheon as proof of their authority. In Suffolk, this contingent of volunteer law-enforcers included butchers, farmers and other agricultural workers.

Suffolk's reliance on this rudimentary system of parish constables was not out of keeping with the small, isolated, rural communities that defined the county until the 1830s. But with sweeping industrialisation, significant population growth and the widespread migration of workers away from the countryside, it was recognised that the police service needed to modernise and become a more professional organisation with paid uniformed officers; one that was better able to deal with some of the social unrest caused by technological transformation and changing economic conditions.

The 1830s and '40s saw the first attempts to establish a professional policing structure in Suffolk, centred on a number of individual force areas. These covered the east and west of the county, Ipswich, Bury St Edmunds, Sudbury, Beccles and Southwold. But the new arrangements would take time to bed down and officer discipline, in particular, would remain a consistent problem throughout the Victorian era.

Working conditions for Suffolk's police officers were tough. Hours were long – twelve to sixteen hours a day – and there were no recognised breaks. Constables were required to wear their uniforms at all times outside of their homes and could be docked pay for minor irregularities like poor spelling. They could not even marry without the permission of their superiors. Among the rules of an officer's appointment were the requirements to act with 'moderation and humanity' and to perform the role 'without malice and partiality'. A local constable was expected to keep the peace, capture those committing crime, and transfer them up to the Quarter Sessions or whatever court was sitting for trial.

The role was also not without its dangers, as the deaths of two officers in the mid-nineteenth century serve to demonstrate. The first occurred in Gisleham on the night of Sunday, 30 July 1844. PC James McFadden had been given the routine job of guarding some farm buildings and in carrying out the task encountered a gang of armed burglars who shot him and left him for dead. McFadden was able to identify his attackers before passing away and the gang were quickly arrested and tried for the crime. Found guilty, gang-leader William Howell was hanged in Ipswich on

25 January 1845. His brother Walter, and accomplice Israel Shipley, were also convicted, but had their sentences commuted. In due course, both were transported for life to Van Diemen's Land (modern day Tasmania).

Police Constable Ebenezer Tye was also to pay the ultimate price at the hands of a burglar. He was stabbed to death in 1862 while bravely trying to apprehend John Ducker in Halesworth. He is buried locally in a spot known as the 'Policeman's Grave'. Ducker was hanged for the crime in Ipswich on 14 April 1863 – the last person to be publicly executed in Suffolk.

The local police establishment in 1864 amounted to less than 300 officers and the number of crimes recorded in that year stood at only 272. And while the number of officers would grow exponentially in the sixty years to follow, so too would the number and range of crimes they were required to investigate. The efficiency of the three separate forces that continued to operate across the county was enhanced at the start of the twentieth century by improved communications (the telephone) and transportation (the bicycle). The Ipswich Borough Force formed its own branch of mounted officers in 1909 and the use of privately-owned motor vehicles by senior officers also began in that year – the first officer to make use of a car being Superintendent W.A. Newson (*see* Chapters 6 and 7), who had just bought a locally-made Anglian two-seater with a De Dion engine.

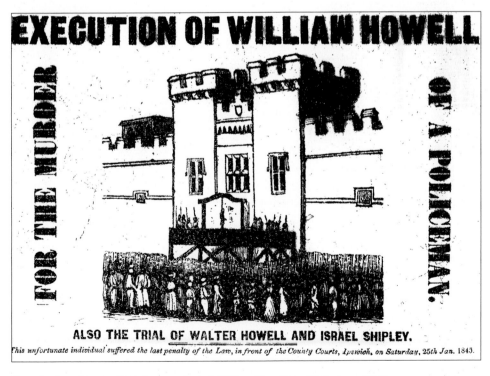

EXECUTION OF WILLIAM HOWELL

FOR THE MURDER

OF A POLICEMAN.

ALSO THE TRIAL OF WALTER HOWELL AND ISRAEL SHIPLEY.

This unfortunate individual suffered the last penalty of the Law, in front of the County Courts, Ipswich, on Saturday, 25th Jan. 1845.

Part of a broadsheet sold at the execution of William Howell on 25 January 1845.

The 'Policeman's Grave' of PC Ebenezer Tye, killed in action while bravely trying to apprehend burglar John Ducker in Halesworth in 1862. (Halesworth Museum)

The period would also be marked by the growing professionalism and capabilities of the constabulary in solving difficult crimes and its increasing reliance on forensic and medical science to secure convictions. Its success in solving the small number of murder cases that arose from time to time was impressive for a rural force of its size.

This collection brings together some of the more significant of these murder cases from Suffolk's criminal past. All have been researched from original source materials and contemporary accounts, including court records, inquest testimonies and press reports. Each has been chosen because it sheds some light on the nature of criminality in days gone by or because it illustrates how the criminal justice system was adapting to the challenges of detecting, convicting and sentencing those who were believed to be guilty of murder. In some cases, the book questions how robust the system was in ensuring that justice was done.

Murder is never a pleasant business and in presenting the material contained within this volume I have tried to reflect the terrible, often devastating impact that the crime can have on individuals, families and the community at large. Wherever possible, I have attempted to position each murder in its social setting, exposing some of the prevailing attitudes of the day and illustrating how media coverage both helped and hindered the pursuit of justice. In all cases, I hope I have avoided sensationalising or glorifying the act of killing.

Mark Mower, 2011

1

KILLED BY POACHERS

Elveden, 1850

Poaching, like smuggling, has a long history in Suffolk and the legal archives are littered with examples of career poachers who continually flouted the established game laws. While the crime was traditionally reviled by those upholding the laws of the land, many others were content to dismiss it as the legitimate right of any country dweller to put food on his table. Yet, as history shows, the nefarious activities of a minority of poachers could sometimes lead to conflict and, occasionally, even death.

Throughout the nineteenth century there continued to be tough penalties for those found guilty of poaching, although the crime was endemic in many parts of the county. In fact, a quarter of all convictions in Suffolk during the 1840s were for game offences. The Black Act of 1723 had made poaching with a blackened face a capital offence for which hanging had become the established punishment. Just being caught in possession of poaching equipment could often result in a year in prison or, at worst, transportation. All of this made the night-time activities of the poachers a deadly serious pursuit, as gamekeeper William Napthen was to discover to his cost on Friday, 20 December 1850 on the Elveden Hall estate.

The village of Elveden is situated deep in the Suffolk countryside in the heart of Thetford Forest. The settlement was first recorded as the Saxon 'Eluedena', meaning a valley inhabited by fairies or elves. An entry in the Domesday census of 1086 reveals that the village had at that time some forty inhabitants engaged in farming, fishing and wildfowling, with one of three Norman-held estates being recorded as Elveden – or Elden – Manor. By the sixteenth century this had become the main manorial settlement and at the time of the Reformation was given by Henry VIII to the Duke of Norfolk.

Passing through successive generations of landed gentry, the Elveden Hall estate was eventually purchased in 1813 by William Newton, a wealthy merchant who had made his fortune trading in the West Indies. Continuing its long history, he maintained many of the open and forested lands of the 1,000-acre estate for game shooting, obtaining all appropriate game licenses and employing a number of professional gamekeepers. One of their roles was to keep a keen eye out for a perennial inhabitant of the local countryside – the village poacher.

Around 10.30 p.m. on the fateful night, a thin layer of mist hung above the open areas of the estate. And while the moonlight had made visibility good in the earlier part of the evening, the sky had since darkened as a result of some sporadic cloud cover – all in all, a good evening for some undercover poaching.

Brothers Isaac and Thomas Allen, who lived and worked on the estate with their father John, were aroused at that time by the loud report of a shotgun. Both men jumped up instinctively and left the cottage without delay, heading off in the direction of an area known as the George IV plantation, about half a mile from their home. As an assistant gamekeeper, Isaac knew only too well that the shot had signalled poachers at work; in recent days, the estate workers had received a tip off that a number of poachers would be venturing onto the estate that night to pursue their illicit trade.

Alongside his brother Thomas, a stable worker, Isaac reached the plantation not long after, and the two were then joined by their father John. Spreading out, the men followed their instincts in heading towards the likely exit points from the grove. They then heard a further shot, followed by the sound of many feet running on the hard ground.

When the poachers broke cover, the estate workers were in close pursuit, joined at that time by a night watchman called Jonathan Jessup. In the uncertain light, they could see their quarry – six poachers in all – heading off across Little Heath towards the Boundary Bank at the edge of the estate and in the direction of Eriswell Grove. None of the workers were armed with anything more than a small bludgeon or stick.

Thomas Allen took the lead at this point and followed the poachers up onto the Boundary Bank. He met with an unequivocal challenge. A man dressed in a long dark coat with a white handkerchief covering his face turned towards Allen and, stepping forward two or three yards, levelled a shotgun directly at him. The man then said in a hoarse voice, 'You bastards, if you don't go back, we'll shoot you.' Allen edged backwards and waited for his colleagues to catch him up, watching the poachers continue in the direction of Eriswell. He noted that at least one other poacher had been carrying a shotgun.

It was at this stage that the estate workers were joined by the head gamekeeper, William Napthen. Isaac Allen quickly assessed the situation and, noting that there were now five of them, turned to Napthen and said, 'Master, let's go at them.' His plan met with no resistance and the group once again set off after the poachers. They were now over 3½ miles from Elveden Hall.

The chase continued for another quarter of a mile, with John Allen trailing behind the others. Within ten yards of their quarry, the four estate workers made a rush at the six men. Almost simultaneously, there were three shots from the poachers' guns – one believed to be a double-barrelled shotgun. One blast had an immediate and fatal impact on Napthen, who collapsed having been shot through the heart and lungs. A second shot missed the estate workers altogether, while the third wounded Isaac Allen in the left hand and arm. But it did not prevent him from falling upon the poachers alongside his brother.

Thomas Allen began to wrestle with the man he believed had shot at his brother. His father, John, reaching the others just after the shooting, was attacked by the poacher who had shot and killed Napthen. The injured Isaac Allen brought the heavy stick he was carrying down across the shoulders of another man while observing one of the poachers stoop to pick up a stone. The brief confrontation ended with a shotgun being broken over John Allen's shoulder. The poachers then fled, pursued only by Thomas Allen, who continued after them for some time until he heard one of the poachers talk about reloading. He then gave up the chase and returned to the scene of Napthen's demise.

The estate workers were grief-stricken by Napthen's death and desperate to track down the culprits. While assaults and injuries to gamekeepers were by no means uncommon at this time, it was rare for poachers to commit murder in making their escape. Napthen's body was carried to the Cornwallis Arms Inn in Eriswell, while Isaac Allen was helped back to his parent's cottage. His wounds were severe, but not life-threatening. Messages were sent to the local surgeon and to the nearby police houses – the estate workers doing their best to describe the assailants in their dispatches. The same information was also sent to nearby railway stations to prevent the suspects fleeing by rail. A tracking party was assembled early the next morning to follow what remained of the poachers' trail. This included a few local police officers, the three Allens and a number of other workers from the estate.

In the early light of the Saturday morning, with the white hoar frost preserving the imprints of the poachers' footfall, the party made good progress in following the trail for several miles through Eriswell and to within a quarter of a mile of Wilde Street in Mildenhall. Here the footprints indicated that the poachers had paused for a while in a field near a scattered hamlet of houses. The presence of pheasant feathers on the ground suggested that some division of the night's booty had taken place.

The poachers had followed a pretty direct route towards this spot. And while the rising sun had removed the overnight frost, making it difficult to continue the pursuit, the tracking party believed that the poachers had been heading towards the Isleham ferry. Beyond this lay the village of Isleham in Cambridgeshire, some 14 miles by road from Elveden. The police officers within the party took the decision to head towards the village to continue the hunt.

At that time, Isleham was a large and scattered Fenland village with three main streets, a population of just over 2,000 inhabitants and less than 500 properties. It was also reputed to be home to a determined community of around forty poachers who made a living from their illicit trade during the winter months when seasonal agricultural work was hard to come by.

It did not take the constables too long to track down some likely culprits. Four local men were arrested and taken to the White Horse public house. They were scrutinised by the Allen brothers and their father, who confirmed that the apprehended men looked like some of the poachers they had seen the previous night. Two further men were arrested the next day and all six men were lodged at the Station House in Mildenhall. They were William Brown, James Cadman, John Starling, Richard Starling, Frederick Fletcher and Joseph Norman.

A subsequent search of the various properties in which the detained men lived revealed little conclusive evidence. A frockcoat was removed by the police from William Brown's house. In a pocket of this the officers found some fresh blood and a quantity of what looked like pheasant feathers. They also found a copper percussion cap over the fireplace. When James Cadman was apprehended, the pocket of his dark velveteen jacket was also found to contain feathers, which were retained as evidence. Crucially, the investigators found no shotguns, powder or poaching snares.

THE MURDER BY POACHERS AT ELVEDON.

The following are the depositions taken at the inquest on the body of William Napthan :—

Thomas Allen deposed : I live at Elvedon, and am in the service of William Newton, Esq. I knew the deceased, who was head gamekeeper to Mr. Newton, and was about 48 years of age. Last Friday night, about half-past ten o'clock, in consequence of hearing the report of a gun at a distance of about a mile, I immediately made for a plantation in Elvedon, called the "George the Fourth" plantation. My brother and I went together, and when we got there we waited outside the plantation, until my father joined us. He stopped at one corner of the plantation, my brother at the other, and I went up outside of the cover. Whilst I was going up, I heard the report of another gun, and about five minutes afterwards I heard the sound of men running on the land. I made after them, and when I got about 100 yards, I saw Jessup. I also observed several men walking across the Little Heath, about half-a-mile from the plantation. I then joined my brother. The men were about 100 yards off, and I called to them to stop, for I knew we could catch them. One of the men turned round and said, "You b——, if you don't go back I'll shoot you," and levelled his gun at us. The deceased came up just after this, my father accompanying him. We were then of the following party : the deceased, Jessup, a watcher, myself, my brother, and my father. We all set out in pursuit of them. We had been after them about an hour before we

A newspaper headline at the time of the murder. (Bury & Norwich Post)

The small community around Elveden was shocked by the death of the gamekeeper and the murder was reported both locally and nationally. Described in various press reports as being forty-seven or forty-eight years of age, William Napthen had been born to parents William and Sarah Napthen in the first decade of the nineteenth century (the 1841 census suggests that he was born in 1808). He left behind him a widow, Maria, and an eighteen-year-old son, William. The gamekeeper had worked on the estate for nearly eighteen years and was well regarded by all of his employer's family and the other estate workers. A short piece in the

Bury & Norwich Post a few days after the murder provided some insight into the nature of the man:

> Napthan [*sic*] was a man of excellent character, not only of sober and industrious habits, but of religious principles – a peace-maker – though his vocation, as the event has unhappily proved, was rather of a warlike character – a friend to his poorer neighbours when in want of assistance, having saved a little property by his frugality; and withal an excellent keeper and a faithful and respectful servant.

On the evening of Monday, 23 December, an inquest was held in the Newton Arms in Elveden before Harry Wayman, coroner for the Liberty and Borough of Bury St Edmunds. The foreman of the jury was Colonel Peel, a Newmarket racehorse owner related to Sir Robert Peel. The inquest heard evidence from the Allen brothers and Thetford surgeon H.W. Bailey, who confirmed that Napthen's death had resulted from the gunshot wounds to his heart and lungs, which had caused an 'effusion of blood'. He believed the death had been instantaneous. The jury returned a verdict of 'wilful murder against several persons unknown.'

A hearing by local magistrates took place the following morning – Christmas Eve – at the Station House in Mildenhall. They took depositions from a number of people in connection with the murder, including the Allen brothers and police surgeon Bailey. William Napthen was laid to rest two days later in the grounds of St Andrew and St Patrick's parish church in Elveden.

The earlier depositions were read out at the start of a second hearing on Monday, 6 January 1851. The six Isleham men appeared before the magistrates on the charge of murdering gamekeeper William Napthen and having shot at and wounded under-keeper Isaac Allen with intent to murder. All of the men denied the charges.

Without other conclusive evidence, it was clear from the outset that much of the case would hinge on the testimony of the estate workers being able to establish, with certainty, that the six men they had seen and chased on the night of the murder were the same individuals that now sat before the magistrates. Thomas Allen deposed that the man who had aimed a shotgun at him on top of the Boundary Bank, while threatening to shoot the estate workers, was William Brown. He claimed that Brown was about the same height as the man he had seen and had a distinctive, rough sounding voice similar to that he had heard. The other men looked about the same height as the poachers he had seen.

In his account, Isaac Allen said that he believed it was Richard Starling who had shot at him, injuring his hand and arm. He described

The Old Shire Hall in Bury St Edmunds, where the trial of the poachers began on Friday, 4 April 1851.

his attacker as having light hair, similar to Starling's. He also believed that it was William Brown who had shot Napthen and described the gunman as wearing a dark coat with 'something dark around his neck.' James Cadman looked like the man he had seen stooping to pick up a stone and John Starling looked like the man he had struck with his stick during the scuffle. The latter was described as wearing a light coat and a cap.

Jonathan Jessup backed up the evidence of his estate colleagues. To the best of his belief, he thought William Brown was the man he had seen shouting the threat and shooting at William Napthen. He also claimed to have seen James Cadman and Frederick Fletcher a number of times that night. Re-examined, he testified that he could not place any of the three remaining prisoners on the estate that night, even though he claimed once to have worked with Richard Starling on the Mildenhall River.

Throughout the testimony, the prisoners challenged the witnesses' accounts and maintained their innocence with some theatricality. At one point, William Brown declared, '...the blessed Lord knows I am as clear as an angel in Heaven. I never wore a frock coat in my life.'

A number of witnesses then testified about events earlier that day. PC Charles Scholefield explained how he had been on duty in Mildenhall at around half-past seven that evening. He had met six men heading out of the town in the direction of Elveden. Four were dressed in dark frock coats, with two others in fustian frocks. It was his belief that William Brown and John Starling were two of the group. Cross-examined, the officer said he could not see if any of the men had any guns or sticks, although he ventured that one man had put something in his pocket and that individual looked like Joseph Norman, although he had not been able to see the man's face.

The prisoners merely declared that they had not been there and, led by William Brown, a couple announced that they had never worn frock coats. Scholefield then went on to describe his search of Brown's house on the Monday following the murder. The coat he had seized with feathers in the pocket was presented to the magistrates. An argument ensued about the nature of the feathers, with Brown declaring that they were lark feathers and another witness stating that he believed them to be pheasant and partridge feathers.

John Theobald, a gamekeeper from Mildenhall, also claimed to have seen a group of men walking towards Elveden on the evening in question. He was on the Elveden road between half-past seven and eight o'clock and was first passed by two men going up the hill opposite his house, about half a mile from Mildenhall. Approximately 100 yards behind the pair were two more men heading in the same direction, with a fifth man some 40 or 50 yards behind them. While talking to a neighbour a short while later, he saw a sixth and final man walk past.

Given his professional role, Theobald had been suspicious of the men's intentions and had followed them for about a mile-and-a-half to ensure that they did not loiter on the estate he was responsible for. He described the first two individuals as wearing dark jackets in which the men appeared to be holding something stiff like a gun or bludgeon. The following pair had worn lighter jackets with the man closest to him again looking to have something stiff in his pocket, as it stuck out like the others. He remembered the two stragglers as wearing dark dress coats.

Theobald further testified that he had not recognised any of the men. The closest he came to identifying any of them in the dock was when he confirmed that the last individual he had seen that evening had appeared to 'lollop' along, rolling from side to side. James Cadman was asked to walk to the door of the courtroom. Having done so, Theobald said that he was about the height of the man he had seen on the night of the murder.

When John Allen was called to give evidence, he again described the events leading to the shooting of William Napthen. This added little to the testimony already given by his sons. However, he then went on to describe how the tracking group had followed the footprints of the six poachers at first light the next morning. His account was backed up by William Leeks, another estate worker.

Police Constable John Etheridge then described the arrest of James Cadman and the search of his Isleham cottage. When he produced the feathers found in Cadman's velveteen jacket, the arguments about their provenance began once more. Cadman maintained that they were lark feathers, while John Theobald and another gamekeeper were called to testify that some appeared to be more consistent with the plumage of pheasants.

The magistrates then asked for the prisoners to be removed from the courtroom, before calling each back in turn to give statements in their own defence. James Cadman was the first to be called. He merely stated that he knew nothing about the events that night and was 'as innocent as the babe unborn.' He had apparently asked for a William Raven to appear in his defence but, when called, the witness failed to materialise.

Next up was Joseph Norman; he had nothing to say, but did call on two witnesses who testified to seeing him at home on the night of the murder. Richard Starling was also able to provide a strong alibi, with four witnesses giving evidence that he was at home that evening.

When asked to give an account of his whereabouts, William Brown told the magistrates that he had been playing dominoes at his house with a William Johnson. He rose at 5.30 a.m. the next morning. He said he knew this because his next door neighbour, Benjamin Andus, had told him the time. When called as a witness, Andus confirmed that he had been in his yard on the Saturday morning – although he gave the time as somewhere between 4 and 5 a.m. – and said that he had heard Brown call from his bedroom window, asking what the time was. He went on to say that he had seen Brown at home between seven and eight o'clock the previous evening.

A second witness, Sarah Payne, claimed to have seen both James Cadman and William Brown that same evening. She had apparently visited the house of Brown's mother and had seen Cadman, his wife and child sitting in the chimney corner of the cottage just before eight o'clock (the testimony also revealed that Brown was Cadman's brother-in-law). She claimed then to have gone next door to visit Brown's wife, who was expecting a child, where she had seen the couple in their home. In the latter part of her testimony, Payne said that she had returned from town around 10 p.m. that evening and, seeing a light on, had tapped at the window of Brown's house before having a conversation with him.

Frederick Fletcher's defence was more straightforward. He claimed to have spent the evening in the Isleham Cock public house in the company of two friends, both of whom testified to this. His father, George, also testified that his son had arrived home just before ten o'clock that night.

When he addressed the magistrates, John Starling said he did not know what to say, other than he 'had nothing to do with it.' Although two witnesses were called in his defence – both saying that they had seen or heard him at home that evening – Starling appeared nervous and unsure of how to conduct the questioning of the witnesses.

Having heard from each of the prisoners, the magistrates then began to discuss the evidence they had heard. Excluded from the courtroom, the six accused men could be heard singing loudly, described later by one of the local reporters as 'apparently very merry,' and adding that, 'For a long time prior to the examination they had been conducting themselves in a similar manner.' This, and their high jinks during some of the earlier exchanges with witnesses, suggested that the men had been drinking prior to the hearing.

The gravestone of gamekeeper William Napthen in the grounds of St Andrew and St Patrick's parish church in Elveden. (Gravestone Photographic Resource)

When they had reached their decision, the magistrates had the doors to the courtroom reopened and when all of the prisoners were again reassembled, the chairman of the bench, Mr Waddington, announced that they had decided to commit William Brown, James Cadman and John Starling for trial at the next assizes. As a result of the alibis given for the other men, they were to be released without charge.

There can be little doubt that the decision to discharge three of the accused on the basis of what had been heard was a serious blow to the authorities. Nevertheless, the police continued to try and build the case against the remaining three men. The following day, it was reported that a reward of £100 had been offered for information about the murder. Half of this was being offered by William Newton – the owner of Elveden Hall – with the remaining £50 being put up by the government. There was also the offer of a pardon for any accomplice who was prepared to give evidence against the person who had fired the fatal shot. In the event, no one came forward to claim either the reward or the pardon.

The three Isleham men were housed in Bury St Edmunds gaol until their trial at the Lent Assizes on Friday, 4 April 1851, before Lord Chief Justice John Jervis. The case for the prosecution was conducted by a Mr Prendergast and a Mr Power. The prisoners were defended by a Mr Palmer.

The early part of the proceedings was taken up with the evidence of the various estate workers who had chased the poachers on the night of the murder. At times the men were challenged by Mr Palmer about what they claimed to have seen. He referred them back to their earlier depositions to the magistrates, pointing out small discrepancies in the testimony they were now giving. The effect was to call into question the reliability of their recollection of events and what they could or could not have seen, given their proximity to the poachers in the less than perfect visibility at the time.

John Gowers, a local postman, said that he had seen William Brown and James Cadman at about half-past four that afternoon. He claimed that they had with them some poles and a net and when he had asked them if they were going out after larks, the pair had answered 'Yes.' PC Charles Scholefield and gamekeeper John Theobald repeated their testimony about seeing a group of poachers in the early evening. Evidence was also given by William Nunn and Thomas Dennis, both from Mildenhall, who remembered seeing the group at that time, although neither could swear on the identity of the men. While useful circumstantial evidence, the various accounts did not constitute a watertight case against the three men sitting in the dock. Similarly, with no fresh forensic evidence to present, the prosecution was forced to rely on the testimonies of the police officers who had searched the properties of the three prisoners in the aftermath of the murder and the few items that had been found.

The testimony of some of the members of the tracking party who had pursued the poachers in the direction of Isleham also did little to strengthen the case. When one witness described seeing signs of where pheasants had fallen from the trees on the estate and finding bits of paper which looked to have been loaded with the shot from a gun, the trial judge dismissed the evidence as unimportant. He reminded the court that they were not trying a poaching case, but a charge of murder.

When the case for the prosecution had been made, Mr Palmer said that he would restrict his remarks to the question of identity. He pointed out that none of the witnesses had given a positive identification and the Allens and Jonathan Jessup, the night watchman, had all said only that they *believed* the prisoners to be the men they had seen. He then pointed out some inconsistencies in their testimonies at the trial compared to those given at the earlier hearing.

The feathers found by the police in the clothing of two of the accused men were dismissed as being evidence only of lark hunting. In short, Mr Palmer pointed out to the jury that the prosecution's case rested on the 'loose and contradictory statements of the keeper's assistants' and was 'of so slight a character that he felt sure they would never upon it consign one or more men to an ignominious death.' He finished by saying that the court had heard earlier that other parties had been discharged by the magistrates because of the strength of their alibis. This evidence, he contended, could equally have applied to the prisoners at the bar.

In summing up, the trial judge said that the case hinged on whether the jury believed the prisoners had been satisfactorily identified. The evidence of feathers found in the pockets of two of the witnesses could be discounted – while this may have been evidence of poaching, it was not evidence of murder and it did not prove that any individual had been out that particular night. He also reminded the jury that three other men had been discharged on the basis of similar evidence heard at the earlier Magistrates Court.

The jury returned after an hour's deliberation to deliver its verdict of 'Not guilty' in favour of all three men. While there was some attempt at applause in the public gallery, this was quickly suppressed. A further charge of night poaching against the men was also dropped the next day, the judge explaining that the defendants would not be asked to testify as the prosecution believed that the jury was unlikely to find them guilty on the basis of the evidence already presented at the murder trial. William Brown, James Cadman and John Starling were all subsequently discharged.

As terrible as the death of William Napthen was, it would not be the last time that one of the estate's gamekeepers would be murdered by a poacher. Nineteen years after the first killing, the small community around Elveden was shocked once more to learn of a similar crime.

In 1863, Elveden Hall was purchased by Prince Duleep Singh, the last Sikh Maharajah of the Punjab, who transformed the estate into a favoured hunting ground for the Victorian elite. The Prince had been born in India in 1838 and was brought to England as a young boy, becoming friends with the British Royal Family, establishing himself within London society and converting to Christianity. He settled into the life of an English country gentleman with apparent ease, rebuilding the stately home and restoring the parish church in Elveden at great cost and to great acclaim. By March 1869, he had also become a magistrate for the West Suffolk area and a respected member of the Suffolk gentry. The estate was stocked with game of all sorts and among the regular visitors to his organised shoots was the Prince of Wales, the future King Edward VII. On one occasion, a six-gun hunting party shot a total of 8,312 head of game in one six-day period on the estate.

All of this required a large staff and Duleep Singh employed experienced men to manage his estates and protect the large number of grouse, pheasants and partridges raised especially for his shooting parties. One of these was gamekeeper John Hight, a nineteen-year-old man who was well known to the small fraternity of local poachers who took their chances in illegally trapping and shooting game on the estate. Always carrying a stick and wearing his characteristic seal skin cap, Hight was also well known and well liked in the small community around Elveden.

The murder occurred on Friday, 31 December 1869. That afternoon, two local men, James Rutterford and David Heffer, had ventured onto the estate with a shotgun in pursuit of game which they planned to sell the next day in Mildenhall. Having bagged some birds, the poachers were heading for home through some woodland when they were pursued by

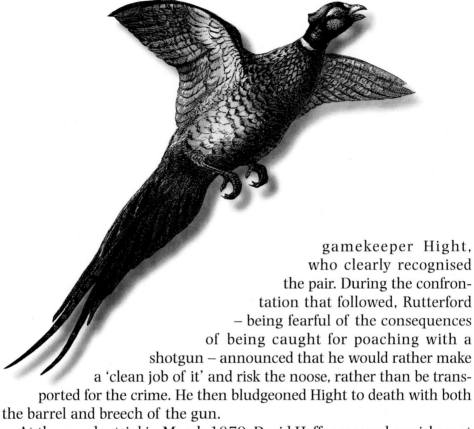

gamekeeper Hight, who clearly recognised the pair. During the confrontation that followed, Rutterford – being fearful of the consequences of being caught for poaching with a shotgun – announced that he would rather make a 'clean job of it' and risk the noose, rather than be transported for the crime. He then bludgeoned Hight to death with both the barrel and breech of the gun.

At the murder trial in March 1870, David Heffer escaped punishment when he turned Queen's Evidence and testified against his partner in crime. And while James Rutterford was found guilty and sentenced to be hanged, he received a last minute reprieve much to the chagrin of the local population. With only thirty-six hours to go before his planned execution, the poacher's sentence was commuted to one of penal servitude for life when it was decided that it would be 'unsafe' to hang him given the extensive scarring on his throat – the result of a severe burn earlier in his life. In the event, Rutterford died within the walls of Pentonville Prison in London less than three years later.

Both of the Elveden murder cases serve only to highlight the absurdity of the laws governing poaching at that time, which turned many countryfolk into hardened criminals for pilfering a small amount of game while rich landowners continued to slaughter excessive quantities of wildlife as a legitimate country pursuit.

2

AN EXTRAORDINARY CASE OF LIFE AND DEATH

Thrandeston, 1851

Jealousy can be a powerful and destructive force, particularly when combined with infatuation and the overwhelming desire to possess and control. So it was that when Mary Baker began working for John Mickleburgh in the early part of 1848, she was to become the focus of his unhealthy desires and violent passions. It was an obsession that would lead to forty years of untold heartache and ultimate pain.

Mary Baker worked as a general domestic servant and dairymaid at Lodge Farm, the estate of John Mickleburgh. The forty-one-year-old farmer owned 27 acres of land and rented a further 16 acres in and around the small village of Thrandeston in the Hartismere Hundred, 3½ miles north-west of the Suffolk town of Eye. He also owned a number of cottages which were rented out to local tenants.

The farmer was 5ft 6in tall and of slim build. He had a long face with a sallow complexion, a large full mouth and dark brown hair. His small eyes were light hazel in colour and set below a rather prominent brow, all of which gave him a slightly wild look. He was married with three children, however, this did not stop Mickleburgh from courting his new employee as soon as she arrived.

Mary was a competent and diligent worker. A later press report described the twenty-one-year-old maidservant as 'possessed of very considerable personal attractions, and of a lively disposition.' She was the youngest of seven children born to parents James and Elizabeth Baker in the Norfolk village of Shelfanger, some 5 miles north of Thrandeston,

SHELFANGER CHURCH

A nineteenth-century engraving of All Saints' parish church in Shelfanger, where Mary Baker was baptised and later buried. (Image courtesy of Norfolk County Council Library and Information Service)

and was baptised in the local church of All Saints on 18 July 1830. Mickleburgh himself had family connections in the village and owned some of the cottages there.

From the outset the couple's relationship was a tempestuous affair and it was clear from later accounts that Mickleburgh's wife, Frances (known as 'Fanny'), had some suspicions that her husband was carrying on with the maidservant. Whether it was through choice, or at the insistence of her lover and employer, Mary left the farm in September 1849 and went back home to her parents. However, a year later she returned, resuming her old job and settling into a relationship with William Bootman, a local journeyman brick maker.

As would be demonstrated by his later conduct, John Mickleburgh was a tough and unyielding character, prone to wild and unexpected mood swings – at times gripped by sudden fits of passion and elation, while just as easily slipping into long bouts of inactivity and despair. Those close to him had grown accustomed to watching for the signals and anticipating his behaviour, which could be both harsh and eccentric. That he was still consumed by his affections for Mary Baker soon became apparent and within a short time the pair had begun to sleep together whenever the opportunity presented itself. Their last liaison occurred on the night of Wednesday, 23 July 1851, when Fanny Mickleburgh had gone off for the evening to visit relatives in Diss.

Whether Mary had called a halt to their affair just after this we may never know, but later events would suggest that this had indeed been the case. Her family had begun to suspect that the two were close, although, when asked, Mary had repeatedly denied that anything was going on between them.

Just over a week later, Mary made plans to attend Thrandeston Fair with William Bootman, her sister Clara and brother-in-law John French. The lamb and cattle fair was a lively two-day event which began on 31 July each year and was held on the village green only half a mile from the Mickleburgh farm. It drew large numbers of visitors from across the county and offered a wide variety of exhibits, stalls and attractions. Domestic staff in the area viewed it as a general holiday, one which pro-vided them with a rare opportunity to let off steam, drink and socialise. Mary arranged to attend the fair on the first day – a Thursday – with the consent of Fanny Mickleburgh, agreeing to return to Lodge Farm no later than 9.30 p.m.

On the day itself, twenty-eight-year-old Clara French came to collect her sister and the pair left the farm at around 3.30 p.m. that afternoon to walk to the fair. Having spent about half an hour wandering around the various exhibits and stalls, they were then joined by Mary's sweetheart William Bootman. Unbeknown to the three of them, John Mickleburgh had also set out from the farm having learnt that Mary was to meet up with Bootman. In a fit of jealousy he aimed to track her down and find a way of stealing her away from his love rival. When he encountered the group five minutes later, he kept his temper under control and his true intentions hidden, good-naturedly inviting the trio to join him for some refreshments in a drinking booth at the fair.

Mickleburgh treated the group to some brandy, wine and beer and ordered more drinks when Clara's husband John French joined them in Eastaugh's booth. He seemed particularly keen to encourage Bootman to drink what was on offer, hoping, no doubt, to render him intoxicated and make his own pursuit of Mary Baker a somewhat easier task. In the event, young Bootman resisted the temptation and some time after 6 p.m. that evening he and Mary left the booth and headed off to another drinking establishment. Just before they did so, Mickleburgh asked Mary casually what time his wife expected her to be back at the farm. She replied, 'About half-past nine.'

Clara French also left the booth just after this and headed for home. Her husband continued to drink with Mickleburgh, but promised to be home not long afterwards. When he failed to appear some fifteen to twenty minutes later, Clara set out to find him. He was still tucked away in the drinking booth with Mickleburgh. Having encouraged the pair to leave, Clara walked with them back into the hurly burly of the fair, explaining within the hearing of Mickleburgh that her sister and William Bootman had headed for a public house known locally as Barrett's bough house.

Mickleburgh then turned to John and announced that he needed to talk to Clara in confidence. He was clearly agitated and when French had stepped forward out of earshot, Mickleburgh demanded that Clara tell her sister he wanted her to be home by 9 p.m. He then explained that he would meet Mary in the low meadow adjacent to his farm. Before walking off he announced that if this did not happen he would 'be revenged.' Unsure of the farmer's meaning, but not particularly troubled by his bizarre behaviour, Clara then re-joined her husband and the couple headed for the bough house to meet up with Mary.

Seized by what the prosecuting counsel would later describe as 'a spirit of bloody revenge,' Mickleburgh then sought out a stall selling knives and other weapons. Hurriedly, he purchased a knife for 2s from William Sayer, a licensed hawker at the fair. The weapon was a distinctive French stiletto knife with a highly-polished six-inch blade protected by a spring back. It was also extremely sharp and when opened out was like a dagger. Such a weapon would generally have been used for killing sheep. Sayer had bought the knife from a dealer in Norwich – it was the only one of its type he had for sale.

Meanwhile, within Barrett's tightly-packed bough house, a lively crowd of about forty to fifty customers were enjoying some drinking and revelry. Mary Baker sat next to Bootman in the main room of the public house. Around a small table to one side of them were John and Clara French. Shortly before 8 p.m., Mickleburgh entered the establishment and, spying Mary, exclaimed, 'Ah Mary, I see you!' The young maidservant gave no reply and was not unduly bothered by his appearance. Mickleburgh headed immediately for a back room in the bar, where he discretely opened the stiletto knife and adjusted the spring back of the weapon. Returning less than two minutes later, he sidled up to his lover and calmly, but deliberately, plunged the steel blade into her side.

It was only when the farmer withdrew the knife that Mary realised she had been stabbed. Mickleburgh then announced coldly, 'Now, Mary, you have it now.' Glancing down she saw the long blade in his hand and screamed out in terror, 'I am dead! I am dead!' All faces turned towards Mary and then to Mickleburgh, who continued to stand by her side, the open knife clearly visible in his hand.

John French jumped up and seized Mickleburgh, holding his arms tightly behind him. The two men wrestled and fell to the floor, with French pinning the assailant to the ground. Having heard the commotion, Charles Barrett, the publican, rushed into the room and quickly removed the knife from Mickleburgh's grasp, before hastening off to summon the police. Mary staggered to her feet and ran into the back room of the bar, where she promptly fainted. With the help of her sister Clara and a dumbfounded William Bootman, she was taken to an upstairs room to rest on a bed.

French continued to keep a hold on Mickleburgh until PC John Baker (no relation to the victim) arrived at the bough house a few minutes later. While waiting, he challenged the farmer, asking him pointedly why he had carried out the attack. Mickleburgh replied coolly, 'I meant to do it. I went and bought the knife on purpose.'

When PC Baker entered the bar he found the attacker sitting quietly on a settle beside French, much the worse for drink. He told him that he was charged with having stabbed a young woman and as a result he would have to be taken into custody. Mickleburgh replied defiantly, 'You may take me, and do as you please with me – I have done what I intended to, and I hope I have done it to perfection.' Almost immediately, he added that he wished his arm had been a little stronger, for he 'would have given her three or four more inches of the blade.'

He then began to swear repeatedly and described in crude detail the nature of his relationship with Mary Baker, calling her 'the Queen of Thrandeston' and 'a magnificent woman' and boasting of the intercourse he had had with her. He said that he had always done what he liked with the servant girl since she had lived in his house. Having observed what had occurred earlier and hearing all of this, William Bootman was visibly overcome with emotion. Mickleburgh merely looked across at the brick maker, pointed and called him 'a damned cowardly rascal.'

Police Constable John Sillett arrived not long after to assist his colleague in taking Mickleburgh into custody at the Station House in Eye. Prior to this he had fetched Walter William Miller, a surgeon from Eye – who happened to be at the fair – to attend to the injured woman. Sillett also found the prisoner to be heavily intoxicated and noted that he appeared to show no remorse for what he had done, repeating many of the phrases he had already articulated to PC Baker. Sillett took custody of the stiletto knife used in the attack.

Dr Miller examined Mary Baker in the upstairs room of the bough house. The shawl, dress and stays that she was wearing had been cut through by the knife and the surgeon found a small wound on the lower part of the left-hand side of her chest, about half-an-inch in length. It had been sufficient to cause considerable internal damage, although the full extent of the injuries would only be revealed later. For the moment, Mary clung on to life, remaining in the bed and being attended to by her sister and others from the village.

Locked up in the Station House at Eye and still heavily drunk, Mickleburgh appeared to have few regrets about his assault on Mary Baker. He explained that he had wanted her to be with him at the fair and freely admitted purchasing the stiletto knife as well as describing the sequence of events leading to the attack. Expressing some hopes that she would not recover, he also added that if she did pull through and would still not accede to his proposals, he had 'the best brace of pistols the world could produce.'

His wife Fanny visited him at the Station House around 6 a.m. the next morning. While history has not recorded her thoughts or feelings about the affair, the accounts which have survived suggest that her husband displayed little spirit of contrition and had lost none of his vindictiveness. PC Baker was to testify later that he heard Mickleburgh say, 'You have suspected me before – now you know all about it – if you had died a year or two ago this would not have occurred.'

Later that morning the prisoner was taken before magistrates at the Town Hall in Eye and charged with cutting and wounding with intent to do grievous bodily harm. He was then remanded to appear again three days later and committed to Ipswich Gaol. On the journey to Ipswich, Mickleburgh once again demonstrated his excitable and destructive temperament. While the party escorting him paused for lunch at the White Horse Inn in Stoke Ash, Mickleburgh – who had refused to eat anything – seized a knife from the table and attempted to cut his throat. He was only prevented from doing so by the speedy intervention of his warders. The farmer declared that he would continue to starve himself.

In the meantime, the chairman of the bench, the Revd Thomas Lee French (apparently no relation of Mary's brother-in-law), took matters into his own hands and travelled down to Thrandeston to interview the critically injured maidservant. While suffering tremendous pain, Mary was able to provide a statement about what had happened at the

The Town Hall in Eye, where John Mickleburgh appeared before local magistrates charged initially with cutting and wounding with intent to do grievous bodily harm.

The White Horse Inn in Stoke Ash, where Mickleburgh attempted to cut his throat while being transported to Ipswich Gaol. (White Horse Inn, Stoke Ash)

fair from her bed in Barrett's bough house. The magistrate's intervention was both timely and well-judged. At 4.30 p.m., having provided the deposition, Mary Baker passed away in front of the magistrate, PC Sillett and the assembled carers. The inquiry had now become a murder investigation.

On Sunday, 3 August, Dr Miller carried out a post-mortem on the deceased in the presence of two other local surgeons. Adding to what he had observed on the night of the attack, he now ascertained that the knife wound had been between 4 and 5 inches in depth and had entered the left cavity of the chest between the eighth and ninth ribs. It extended downwards and inwards through the diaphragm and spleen and into the peritoneum. The heart and lungs had not been punctured. It was clear that the injuries had caused a significant loss of blood and the surgeon was able to conclude that the wound had been the cause of death.

At 10 a.m. on the Monday morning, an inquest began in the main bar of Barrett's bough house before coroner Charles Gross. After the jury had been sworn in an attempt was made to view the body in the upstairs bedroom, but this proved impossible given the nauseous odours which now filled the tiny room. At the suggestion of the foreman of the jury, the proceedings were adjourned and resumed a short while later in a large and much more convenient room at the farmhouse of a Mr Saunders, who lived close-by. While he had been transported back from Ipswich Gaol earlier that morning, John Mickleburgh was not called to give evidence. He was awaiting a second appearance before the magistrates in Eye.

The inquest jury heard evidence from William Bootman, John French, PC Sillett and Dr Miller. In his summing up, the coroner said it was his duty to inform them that there could be no doubt about their verdict, which must be one of wilful murder against John Mickleburgh. After deliberating for a quarter of an hour, the jury returned a verdict to that effect.

When Mickleburgh was brought up before the magistrates later that day, the outcome was similarly predictable. The farmer was dressed like a country squire, with a long grey coat, a black cravat, blue trousers striped with white and Wellington boots. In front of a packed public gallery he looked tired and dejected and, when called to stand and answer the charge against him, he fainted and fell to the floor. From then on he appeared to be disinterested in the proceedings, which commenced with the reading of the testimony given by Mary Baker just before her death. Having heard from a range of witnesses, including Dr Miller, Clara French, William Sayer and PCs Brown and Sillett, the magistrates wasted no time in committing Mickleburgh to stand trial on the charge of 'wilful murder'.

The nature of the Thrandeston murder attracted considerable press attention locally and nationally, coming as it did alongside a string of other high-profile murder cases in Suffolk during 1851. This included the trial and execution of George Cant for drowning to death thirty-year-old Elizabeth Bainbridge in the small village of Lawshall in January of that year. In reporting the outcome of the magisterial enquiry into Mary Baker's death, an article in the *Bury & Norwich Post* on Wednesday, 6 August, captured the mood. Under the header 'Horrible Murder at Thrandeston,' the piece opened by saying, 'Another of those dreadful crimes which, within the last six or seven months, have rendered the rural district on the borders of Suffolk and Norfolk so unhappily notorious, has been perpetrated in the village of Thrandeston...'

In contrast, the funeral of Mary Baker – later that same day – received little media attention. In a quiet ceremony conducted by Mr Morris, the local rector, and attended by her close family and the small number of people who had known her, Mary was laid to rest in the graveyard of All Saints' Church in Shelfanger. The burial register for the church records nothing more than the basic details of her burial – nothing, in fact, to indicate the callous way in which her life had been taken away from her so prematurely.

For his part, John Mickleburgh continued to attract the attentions of the press, despite being incarcerated within the County Gaol. The *Ipswich Express* on 17 August was one of a string of papers across the

The County Gaol in Ipswich, where Mickleburgh was held until June 1852.

country which reported that the prisoner had continued to carry out his avowed intention of starving himself, taking no food and living entirely on liquids, such as tea and coffee. Mickleburgh had apparently declared that nothing would induce him to partake of any kind of nourishment, saying that he would never disgrace his family by having it said that he had been hanged in front of Ipswich Gaol. His resolve was clearly not as strong as his stomach, for three days later it was reported that the authorities had remonstrated with the prisoner – that should he obstinately persist in his intention, efforts would be made to force him to take sustenance – and Mickleburgh had 'been induced to partake of food.'

The Lent Assizes opened in Bury St Edmunds in March 1852. They were presided over by Lord Chief Justice John Campbell (1st Baron Campbell). The seventy-three-year-old judge had been a Whig politician and was later to become the Lord Chancellor of Great Britain. The proceedings were to include another high-profile murder case. Eighty-year-old William Rollinson, a farm labourer from Sowley Green near Haverhill, was charged with poisoning Anne Cornell, the sister of his lodger and one-time daughter-in-law, Mary Jermyn. Rollinson used white arsenic powder to poison Jermyn's cooking flour in a bitter dispute over some household furniture. He succeeded in poisoning Jermyn and over twenty others who ate various pastries cooked with the deadly flour. All but Anne Cornell survived the effects of this arsenical poisoning. Found guilty, Rollinson was sentenced to be hanged, although this was later commuted to a prison term for what remained of his life.

Mickleburgh's trial began at the Crown Court on Wednesday, 24 March 1852. He was defended by Mr Prendergast, who had the year before conducted the unsuccessful prosecution of the poachers in the William Napthen murder trial (*see* Chapter One) and Mr Palmer, who had been the defence counsel in the same case. Appearing for the prosecution were a Mr Dasent and a Mr Bulwer.

When he was placed in the dock, John Mickleburgh displayed no visible signs of emotion and in a firm voice pleaded 'Not guilty' to the indictments of both the coroner's inquest and Magistrates Court. Mr Dasent stated the case and then began to call witnesses for the prosecution. What followed was largely a re-run of the damning testimony already presented at the earlier hearings.

William Bootman explained his relationship with the murder victim and gave an account of what had happened at the fair that fateful day. John and Clara French recounted their recollection of events, culminating in the stabbing, while Charles Barrett described hearing the shrieks afterwards and his action in taking the knife away from Mickleburgh. PCs Sillett and Baker gave evidence about the arrest and detention of the farmer, his intoxication and the statements he had made in admitting his guilt and premeditation. They also made it clear that he had shown no sorrow or remorse for his actions.

William Sayer, the hawker, testified to selling a stiletto knife at the fair for 2s which looked like the one presented in evidence at the trial. While he was not able to say whether the prisoner had been the person who had bought it between 7 and 8 p.m. on the night of the murder, he admitted that he did not know of any other stalls at the fair that had sold knives of that particular type.

Surgeon Walter Miller repeated his medical testimony, including the results of the post-mortem examination and his opinion on the cause of death. The case for the prosecution ended with the testimony of Elizabeth

SUFFOLK LENT ASSIZES,

MARCH, 1852.

THE TRIALS

(Before the Lord Chief Justice CAMPBELL)

OF

JOHN MICKLEBURGH,

For the MURDER of MARY BAKER;

WILLIAM ROLLINSON,

For POISONING ANNE CORNELL;

WILLIAM BALDRY,

For ATTEMPTING TO POISON HIS WIFE;

AND OF

GEORGE NORRIS,

For ABDUCTION.

PRICE THREEPENCE.

PRINTED AND PUBLISHED BY

BARKER AND SON, 26, HATTER STREET, BURY.

A published transcript of Mickleburgh's trial at the Suffolk Assizes in March 1852.

French, the sister of Mary's brother-in-law, who had been present when Dr Miller had attended to the injured maidservant. She confirmed that Mary Baker had been the person who had died.

In leading the defence, Mr Prendergast acknowledged that the jury had certainly heard a most melancholy and dreadful narration and did not deny that the proof of the act committed by Mickleburgh appeared pretty clear. In attempting to set up a plea of insanity, he said that he would demonstrate that the prisoner had been placed under circumstances which meant that he could not be held responsible for his conduct.

In calling the various witnesses that followed, the prosecution hoped to convince the jury that from his actions Mickleburgh had been regarded as 'mad and deranged' from an early age and had been the child of a person who herself 'was in a state either of lunacy or insanity, or something nearly approaching it.' In effect, what had driven him to kill that day was the 'maniacal fits' he had suffered from since childhood.

Edward Woolsey was the first to be called. He was a labourer who had worked for Mickleburgh since 1835 and had been a tenant of the farmer for seventeen years. He recounted how his employer had set him to plough one day and had later come into the field to ask what he was up to. When Woolsey reminded him that it was he who had asked for the ploughing to be done, Mickleburgh had apparently said, 'The devil – I did not set you to plough here.' Woolsey had carried on with his work and had later told Mrs Mickleburgh about her husband's conduct. She had allegedly replied, 'Keep on ploughing – your master is not exactly right...' Woolsey went on to testify how Mickleburgh suffered from periodic bouts of melancholia and had often been unable to attend to his business. He also said that on the day of the stabbing he had seen the farmer at 5.15 a.m. that morning attempting to hoe some turnips using the tool like a pickaxe or mattock. When Mickleburgh had turned to face him, he had apparently looked 'very wild and ghastly.'

Charles Barham, another employee, provided further examples of Mickleburgh's eccentricity. He recounted how, in April 1851, he had been present when the family sat down to breakfast one morning. Mrs Mickleburgh had been removing boiled eggs from a saucepan, and her husband had apparently been taking them, rolling them in his hand and throwing them on the fire. At one point he was heard to say, 'Let us burn these little devils.'

Other witnesses were called to shed light on Mickleburgh's odd behaviour during childhood. Ezra Garrard, a schoolmaster from Diss, said that he had known the defendant for forty years and described him as a 'very eccentric and singular boy' who was sometimes 'very much elated, and sometimes very desponding.' Garrard also testified that Mickleburgh's mother had been a strange woman who had been known to sit in a dry ditch in a field for long periods of time for no particular reason.

Mary Read, Mickleburgh's sister-in-law, said she had known him for twenty-five years and had at one time contemplated marrying the farmer. She claimed to have decided against this as she believed that he was 'not sound in his mind' and further testified that 'sometimes he would break out in ungovernable passions, he would kick the table over covered with tea things, and at other times he was low, and would not take any notice of anyone.' She explained how her sister had married Mickleburgh against her advice.

The evidence of Henry Ward, a surgeon based in Diss, was clearly designed to provide expert testimony on Mickleburgh's mental state. He had known his patient since 1835 and had no hesitation in saying that he believed him to have an 'unsound mind'. Unfortunately for the defence, it soon became clear that while the doctor had seen and talked to Mickleburgh at his home on many occasions while tending to the farmer's family, he had only ever treated the man himself twice, and both times this had been for indigestion.

This scant medical knowledge did not prevent the surgeon from putting forward his theories about Mickleburgh's mental health. This included the following testimony:

> There is something in the colour of his skin and expression of his face indicating that he is of unsound mind. His observations were generally those of a man with a diseased mind. I always avoided conversation with him; it was so exceedingly unpleasant from the violence of his expressions and manners. I don't think he is a bad-tempered man. I attribute that violence to a want of controlling power over himself.

More significantly, the surgeon's testimony had the effect of undermining the insanity plea and the contention that Mickleburgh could not be held responsible for his actions at the time of the murder. In responding to a question from the judge, Ward said, 'I believe that insane persons may have correct notions of the distinction between right and wrong; even during the fits they generally have this knowledge.'

When the case for the defence had been concluded, it was no surprise that Mr Dasent should return to the issue of whether Mickleburgh had been able to distinguish between right and wrong at the time he committed the fatal act. He put it to the jury that the defendant's conduct at the fair 'was that of a man determined to carry out a fixed and deadly spirit of revenge.' He also suggested that even if the accounts which had been given did provide evidence of insanity, this did not in itself affect the charge against the prisoner. For that to be the case, he said that the jury must believe that at the time the blow was inflicted, Mickleburgh had indeed not known right from wrong.

In his summing up, Justice Campbell also reminded the jury that this was the fundamental issue facing them and went on at length to explain the legal position regarding pleas of insanity. In summarising the evidence for the defence, he observed that the attempt to show that the prisoner had suffered from 'a taint of hereditary insanity' had been unsuccessful.

The jury needed only a short time to reach its decision. Following a few minutes of consultation, a verdict of 'Guilty' was returned.

When Mickleburgh was called on by the judge to say whether there was any reason why the sentence of death should not be passed upon him, he launched an attack on his own defence:

> If the case had been conducted on the merits, I should have stood right. As it is, instead of being built on a rock of truth, it is built on a pillar of straw. I suspected so from the first. I am not insane. There is no insanity if you had heard the whole truth. I knew how it would be; I knew it from the first. It was no insane thing, and it cannot stand. I like to see the truth blaze out...

At the end of a long address, he concluded by requesting – apparently with some feeling – that the knife used in the attack and produced in court 'might be destroyed' for the 'sake of the young woman.' The speech produced a clamour of applause and some jeering within the courtroom and it took some time for silence to be restored. Justice Campbell then donned the black cap and, against some further protests from Mickleburgh, passed the sentence of death in the customary way. The date of execution was set for Wednesday, 7 April 1852.

Despite the sentence of the court, Mickleburgh did not hang for the murder. Some two weeks after the trial, *The Times* carried a short update on the various appeals that had been made to the Home Secretary following the round of capital convictions that spring. Referring to the case of John Mickleburgh, the paper reported that, 'Although not declared irresponsible for his acts, there is enough ground for inquiry into his general eccentricity, which, coupled with the heat and suddenness of the act, has caused inquiries to be instituted into his state of mind.'

In fact, the appeal against his death sentence had been driven largely by Fanny Mickleburgh, who secured the support of the Anti-Punishment of Death Society in calling for a reprieve. On Saturday, 3 April, a deputation of gentlemen led by Ipswich magistrate J.B. Ross travelled to London to deliver a signed petition to the Home Secretary asking for a commutation on the grounds of insanity. Their efforts were not in vain. At midnight on the Monday, a Queen's messenger arrived at Ipswich Gaol with an official despatch for Mr Alloway, the Prison Governor. It announced an immediate respite. This did not prevent a number of local papers reporting later that week that the death sentence had been carried out.

The guilty man continued to be held in Ipswich Gaol until the full outcome of the commutation was known. On 8 June 1852, it was announced that Mickleburgh was to be transported for life and arrangements were made for him to be moved to Millbank Prison in London. So began the next extraordinary stage of the farmer's life.

From 1843, Millbank Prison, on the north bank of the Thames close to Vauxhall Bridge, was used mainly as a holding facility for all convicted criminals facing transportation to Australia. The prison was built on 16 acres of land purchased from the Marquis of Salisbury in 1799 (Tate Britain is now situated on part of the original site) and cost around £500,000 to construct. When completed in 1821, it resembled

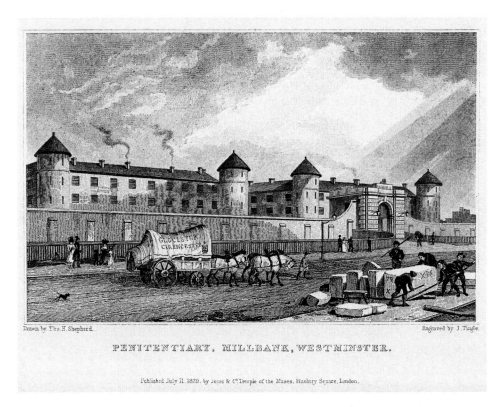

Drawn by Tho. H. Shepherd.   Engraved by J. Tingle.

PENITENTIARY, MILLBANK, WESTMINSTER.

Published July 11. 1829. by Jones & Cº Temple of the Muses, Finsbury Square, London.

An engraving of Millbank Prison in London from 1829. (Wellcome Library, London)

a fortress – the thick external brick walls around the site being arranged to form an irregular octagon. The prison design itself was based on some utilitarian principles identified by the philosopher Jeremy Bentham, and the six internal pentagons of the structure were laid out like spokes around a central area containing the governor's house. At the time, it was the largest prison in Europe and operated until 1890, when it was finally pulled down.

By 1852, the prison was equipped to house around 1,300 male and female prisoners. The main building occupied some 7 acres of the site, alongside the space required for all of the supporting buildings and yards. The remainder of the land was laid out in gardens, which were cultivated by some of the inmates. On arrival at the prison, Mickleburgh would have faced a cold bath and a full medical examination. Having been declared free from any contagious diseases, he would then have been placed on a reception ward before being allocated his own cell. All convicts were issued with a uniform of a blue shirt, a cravat which was blue with a narrow brick-red check, trousers in brown flannel with a thin red stripe, a grey jacket, and a grey Scotch cap.

At that time, around 4,000 convicts were being transported annually from Britain and those awaiting transportation were detained at Millbank for at least nine or ten months. All were kept in solitary confinement and restricted to silence for the first three months of their detention.

This harsh system of enforcement, known as the 'separate system', had been designed to break the spirit of even the toughest convict. Each inmate was locked up in their own cell, in which they would work, rest, eat and sleep, unable to see or speak to anyone other than their prison warder. There was one brief period of exercise in the prison yard each day, but even here the strict rule of silence was enforced. The only other times when an inmate might be permitted to leave his cell was during occasional visits to the prison schoolroom or to attend chapel once a week. But as a non-conformist, Mickleburgh would not even have had this respite.

After three months in solitary confinement, each prisoner was put to work alongside other inmates. While this was seen as an essential element of their penal detention, the tasks also enabled the prison to assess the nature and character of the inmates, the likelihood of their rehabilitation and their suitability for transportation. This was necessary because the Australian colonists, after decades of having to cope with every kind of convict shipped out from Britain, had begun to insist that they would accept only reasonably fit, younger convicts whose characters could be shown to have been reformed, and who could develop into worthy citizens.

In essence, the prison became a convict workshop, with individuals employed in various trades and being allowed to use a portion of their notional earnings for day-to-day necessities. Most of the convicts at Millbank were employed making soldiers' tunics, biscuit-bags, hammocks and the uniforms worn by the prisoners themselves. Others were engaged in weaving or shoe making. A small number, on light duties, received instruction in gardening or were given the mind-numbing task of gathering 'coir' or 'oakum' fibres by untwisting and unpicking lengths of old rope.

As a forty-two-year-old murderer with questionable mental health, Mickleburgh would have been an unlikely candidate for transportation. In fact, for most convicts who were over thirty-five years of age or sick, the assessment period was largely academic as they were unlikely to go to Australia under any circumstances. Having already been reprieved once, Mickleburgh now found himself facing twenty-one years of penal servitude in Millbank. In many respects, this continued to be a death sentence.

For long-term inmates, conditions remained tough and unrelenting. Unless prevented by illness, prisoners were required to work for twelve hours a day, excluding the time allowed for meals. The only exceptions to this were on Sundays, Christmas Day, Good Friday and Thanksgiving. There were 103 prison officers within the penitentiary – an average of one officer for every eleven male convicts – allowing for a high degree of supervision. Rule-breaking would generally lead to the withdrawal of privileges and food, with more serious offences being dealt with by detention in a refractory or darkened cell, being placed in handcuffs or by whipping with a cat or birch.

Food was basic and repetitive. Breakfast consisted of cocoa and 8oz of bread. Dinner comprised 5oz of boiled meat, 1lb of potatoes and 6oz of bread. Supper brought a further 8oz of bread and a pint of gruel, made with oatmeal or wheat flour, and sweetened with molasses.

Each prison cell was 12ft long by 7ft wide. Beneath their solitary cell window, each prisoner had a small table of plain wood, on which would stand a Bible and a small number of other instructional books. There was also a slate and pencil, a wooden platter, tin pint pots for drinking the cocoa and gruel, a salt cellar and a wooden spoon. Below the table would be housed a broom and other daily utensils. A washing tub and wooden stool completed the furniture of the room and a hammock slung from the ceiling allowed each convict to sleep above the cold floor of the cell.

While each cell was well ventilated, the low marshy position of the prison made conditions damp and unhealthy. For the size of its population, Millbank had twice as many cases of illness as Pentonville and nineteen times as many as Brixton Prison. It also had seven times as many deaths as the latter. Outbreaks of cholera were not uncommon and it was only in 1854, two years after Mickleburgh's arrival, that fresh water was pumped into the prison from the artesian wells in Trafalgar Square. Prior to that, the water supply consisted of an immense oval tank fed with the murky water of the Thames.

This then was the environment in which Mickleburgh expected to live out his life. Back home in Thrandeston, his wife Fanny continued to manage Lodge Farm and raise his three daughters. One of the few acts of kindness her husband had undertaken while facing the death penalty was to sign a deed of settlement, transferring the farm and its contents and all of his other lands and properties over to her. She was well regarded locally and considered to be a generous and industrious woman. It is almost certain that she never expected to see her husband again.

Despite the fact that Fanny had sought no legal divorce, she remarried at some point prior to 1869. Her second husband was Thrandeston farmer and overseer Edgar Nunn. In that year, he was recorded in a Post Office Directory as being resident at Lodge Farm and later accounts indicate that he had adopted the name Edgar Mickleburgh-Nunn in recognition of his union with Fanny. Imprisoned within the thick walls of Millbank, John Mickleburgh had no knowledge of his wife's bigamy.

The prison's system of continual surveillance worked to the advantage of some prisoners. Those who were observed to be operating within all of the rules could receive a good conduct badge, which would entitle them to small privileges. Longer-term, the most trustworthy prisoners, who had demonstrated that they were reformed characters, were sometimes given a 'ticket of leave' and – subject to certain conditions – released from prison. This is what happened in Mickleburgh's case. Notwithstanding the nature of the murder and his earlier death sentence, he was released from Millbank having served less than his twenty-one-year sentence. The only restriction placed on him was that he was prohibited from entering the county of Suffolk without the express permission of the Home Secretary.

On leaving prison, Mickleburgh immediately sought permission to travel home and visit his wife and children in Thrandeston. Here he discovered for the first time that Fanny had remarried and the farm was now in the hands of Edgar Nunn. We can only imagine his despair on learning the news. Unable to continue living in the county, he took refuge close by, settling 6½ miles away in the Norfolk village of Winfarthing. At the time of the 1871 census, the sixty-one-year-old was boarding at No.42 Diss Road and working as an agricultural labourer. His landlady and employer was none other than Mary Read, his wife's sister and one of his early lovers. It might be remembered that she had given testimony at the murder trial.

In the ten years that followed, John Mickleburgh continued to live and work in the area, pursuing a trade as a carpenter and wheelwright. By 1881, he was living at No.71 Rectory Road in Shelfanger, the same village that Mary Baker had grown up in many years before. There was a large measure of insensitivity in choosing to settle there, as a number of local papers were later to recognise. But Mickleburgh's story was far from over.

Rectory Road in Shelfanger, Norfolk, where John Mickleburgh was living in 1881.

On Tuesday, 6 April 1887, Fanny Mickleburgh-Nunn died at the age of seventy-four. Her husband, Edgar, was declared bankrupt some months later, but retained possession of Lodge Farm. On 19 September he put the house and estate up for auction in a property sale at Diss. But while the bidding reached £460, it was eventually withdrawn from the sale. It was just as well, for the following month Nunn faced a public examination for his indebtedness – which amounted to almost £400 – and it soon became clear that the land and property were not his to sell. He later made an application to the Ipswich bankruptcy court to be granted an allowance out of the estate, but the judge said he had no legal power to grant such an order, declaring that as the marriage had not been lawful, Nunn had no claim over any part of the estate.

In looking into the background to the story, the *Ipswich Journal* unwittingly discovered that John Mickleburgh – the murderer that most locals believed had been transported to Australia many years before – had been obtaining an honest living less than 10 miles from the scene of his crime for well over fifteen years. However, in deference to his position and the feelings of his family, the paper chose not to report this revelation at the time. Ironically, it was only with the violent and unexpected death of the former convict a few months later that his extraordinary tale was revealed.

While Mickleburgh had continued to work locally, his health had begun to deteriorate. So much so that he had become reliant on some of the outdoor relief provided by the Guiltcross Union, which operated many of the workhouses within the Diss area of Norfolk. In July 1887, he had become too weak and infirm to continue to work outside and the guardians of the Union thought it best to transfer the seventy-seven-year-old to the sick ward of Kenninghall Workhouse at the end of that month.

The workhouse was situated 1½ miles from Kenninghall village and was built in 1836 at a cost of almost £5,000. It was a large, plain building constructed from lump clay and faced with red bricks. While originally built to accommodate 280 inmates, it was later able to house 350, although the institution rarely achieved anything like that level of occupancy.

Throughout the January of 1888, Mickleburgh was suffering from acute bronchitis. He was visited occasionally by Dr Joseph W. Wilson, the Medical Officer, who applied a poultice to his back. The doctor recognised him to be feeble and emaciated, but believed the old man to be rallying well. He was therefore a little surprised to be called to attend the inmate on the morning of Wednesday, 22 February. When he arrived on the sick ward, he found Mickleburgh in bed and breathing with some difficulty.

All that remains of Kenninghall Workhouse in Norfolk, where John Mickleburgh died on 1 March 1888.

The patient seemed to flinch every time the doctor attempted to examine him. He was found to have severe bruising across his chest and extreme tenderness in the pit of his stomach. The Medical Officer did not believe that the injuries were the result of bronchitis and had suspicions that the old man had been punched in the belly and chest.

The sick-room attendant was sixty-one-year-old John Revell Burrows, a partially disabled man who was himself an inmate. When Dr Wilson challenged him about Mickleburgh's condition, the attendant denied hitting the inmate. The Medical Officer then pointed out, 'If you didn't strike him, someone else did.' He reported the matter to James Cole, the Master of Kenninghall Workhouse, who began an investigation later that afternoon.

Cole discovered that Rosetta Rumsby, a nurse on the sick ward, had known about the attack on Mickleburgh but had failed to report it. She had attended to the old man on the morning of 20 February. He was up and dressed and sitting by the fire in the sick ward, complaining of great pains in his chest. A couple of nights later his condition had worsened and he could not lie down properly because of the discomfort. As Nurse Rumsby attempted to put him to bed, Mickleburgh admitted, 'I have had a blow.' But when the nurse asked him who had inflicted the injury, he refused to say.

James Cole soon established that on the night of 19 February there had been a scuffle on the sick ward involving John Burrows. Mickleburgh was known to be very irritable and as a result of his ill-health had required more than the usual amount of assistance from Burrows. The two men had argued and it was believed that Burrows had struck Mickleburgh in the chest and wrestled with the old man on a bed. For the rest of the night his sleep had been disturbed and he complained bitterly of being injured.

When Cole asked Mickleburgh about the bruising on his chest, the old man confirmed that the attendant had attacked him. Responding to the allegation, Burrows continued to maintain his innocence. Cole wasted no time in informing the Board of Guardians about his findings and was instructed to take proceedings against the sick-room attendant. Burrows was duly arrested by the police and taken to a lock-up in East Harling. On Thursday, 1 March, the situation became more serious when it was discovered that John Mickleburgh had finally passed away.

The death was a serious concern for the workhouse, which had only one year before been the scene of a brutal murder. One of the inmates on the sick ward – Jonas Rivett – had risen from his bed on the night of 12 February 1887 and made his way to the room in which Henry Baker, the sick-room attendant, was sleeping. Without rousing Baker, he had stabbed him in the neck, severing his jugular vein and leaving him for dead. The attendant passed away not long after. The seventy-one-year-old inmate was tried for the crime at the Suffolk Assizes on 21 June that year and found guilty. While he was condemned to death, his sentence was later commuted following concerns about his mental health and he was admitted to the Broadmoor Criminal Lunatic Asylum.

An inquest was held in the workhouse on the day after Mickleburgh's death before Mr H.E. Garrod, coroner for the Liberty of the Duke of Norfolk. Three witnesses testified that there had been a scuffle on the night of 19 February and that John Burrows had struck the deceased.

Inmate Edward Leech recalled that Mickleburgh had cried out, 'Pray don't hit me no more, you'll kill me,' and then claimed that Burrows had answered, 'No, no, I shall not kill you.' Mickleburgh had then gone on to say, 'Good Lord have mercy upon me, I must die. You have knocked my stomach in.' Leech added that the old man had groaned for two hours afterwards, praying that he might be spared further pain.

When Dr Wilson was examined he outlined the extent of the injuries he had observed on Mickleburgh's body on the morning of 22 February. He believed that the blow to Mickleburgh's stomach would have accelerated his death, but did not rule out the possibility that the inmate might have died anyway as a result of his bronchitis. In his summing up, the coroner said that while Mickleburgh may have been troublesome, there was no justification for his harsh treatment. After deliberating for only a short while, the decision of the jury was that John Burrows had committed manslaughter and he was committed to stand trial at the next assizes.

The trial at the Norfolk Assizes took place at the Shire Hall in Norwich on Saturday, 14 July 1888. John Burrows was brought to the courtroom

The Shire Hall in Norwich, where John Burrows was tried for the manslaughter of John Mickleburgh in July 1888.

using an underground tunnel that ran from Norwich Castle Prison to the building on Market Avenue. Mr C. Cooper prosecuted and – at the request of the court – Mr F.K. North defended the prisoner.

The prosecution relied on the testimony of the staff and inmates of Kenninghall Workhouse who claimed to have witnessed the crime or who had heard Mickleburgh's denunciation of Burrows. This included the medical testimony of Dr Wilson.

The *Ipswich Journal* was later to report that Mr North gave 'a very able speech for the prisoner.' In doing so, he pointed out the 'unsatisfactory character' of the two aged inmates who claimed to have seen Burrows strike Mickleburgh. He suggested that the bruising afterwards observed on the chest of the deceased might have been caused accidently, when the old man was being lifted in and out of bed, or as a result of his falling against a portion of the bedstead. He went on to say that Mickleburgh had been 'an irritable and provoking old man' who had attempted to knock the pipe out of Burrow's mouth while the attendant was trying to assist him. The prisoner had been forced to hold Mickleburgh's arm to prevent this, and in doing so 'might have unintentionally hurt the inmate, causing him to complain.'

Mr North contended that the prosecution had failed to show that any blow received by Mickleburgh had actually caused his death. Dr Wilson had, after all, said that 'the deceased was in such a condition of health that, at such an inclement season and at such an advanced age, he would not have been surprised any day to have heard that his patient had slipped through his fingers.'

The defence had indeed been well conducted. After its deliberations, the jury returned a verdict of 'Not guilty' and John Burrows walked free. The acquittal attracted little more than a couple of lines in most papers and even the local press accounts were scant in detail. Yet the end of the trial marked the final chapter in what had been an extraordinary case of life and death for a Suffolk farmer whose jealousy and infatuation had led him to commit the horrific murder of a young woman some thirty-seven years earlier.

3

THE SWEETHEART MURDER

Brantham, 1875

The village of Brantham lies along the southern border of Suffolk, close to the River Stour, with extensive views down the valley to the Essex town of Harwich. In the census of 1871, its population numbered just 440, with most inhabitants engaged in farming and trades related to agriculture. The parish covered some 2,000 acres of land, with a further 560 acres of water. Braham Hall – situated in the small hamlet of Cattawade – was one of the more significant properties in the area. The farm estate was widely recognised for its rich arable lands, being once the moated manorial home of Thomas Tusser, a sixteenth-century agricultural writer and poet who penned his 'Hundreth Good Pointes of Husbandrie' while residing there. In 1875, Braham Hall Farm was owned by the wealthy farmer and coal merchant Henry Canham Page, who lived on the estate with his wife and family. In the summer of that year, the family's good name and reputation would be forever tarnished by the violent actions of Henry's twenty-year-old son, Frederick Ernest Page.

Frederick was born in June 1855 and christened on 18 October. He was one of fourteen children born to the Page family. His father was a significant figure within the community, his farm estate covering more than 400 acres and requiring the employment of thirteen men and five boys. Within the hall itself there were three domestic servants tending to the family's needs.

Like his brothers before him, Frederick had received a private education, being a pupil at the Mistley House boarding school on the outskirts

Braham Hall Farm, the Page family home, where Frederick stayed each weekend.

of Manningtree run by headmaster William Holloway Gardner. There are no surviving records to indicate what sort of pupil he was or his level of academic ability, although his later employment suggests that he must have been reasonably numerate and literate. At just over 5ft 7in tall, he was of average height, although some later accounts would describe him as 'undersized'. He had a dark, somewhat pale complexion, with black hair and thick eyebrows. With a slight congenital squint and a persistent speech impediment, he was not given to open or expansive gestures and was occasionally perceived by others to be furtive or sullen.

Frederick had worked for nine months as a clerk for Messrs Lay & Wheeler, the prestigious international wine merchants who operated from No.10 High Street, Colchester (the business, which began in 1854, still thrives to this day and recently became a subsidiary of Majestic Wine Warehouses Ltd). His principal duty was to make entries into the books of the firm. It was an enviable position for a young man with a good education, but it is likely that he secured the job more as a result of his father's connections than his own experience or business acumen. His two previous jobs had ended in disaster and demonstrated clearly his increasing mental health problems.

In 1873, he had been apprenticed to James Robinson, a chemist on Orford Hill in Norwich. Living on the premises, he had taken to staying up until around 2 a.m. each night, groaning and howling like a dog and laughing frequently without reason. At one point, he purchased a brace of pistols and later confessed to his family that he had intended to kill his employer. With the continual disturbances at night, the chemist had been forced to ask Frederick to leave.

The farmer's son next secured a position as a clerk in the goods department of the Great Northern Railway in Kirkstead, Lincolnshire. While there, he tried to commit suicide by placing his head on the railway line and was saved only by the timely intervention of a railway porter.

In Victorian Britain, these symptoms of psychosis were often branded simply as a sign of madness. With little public or professional recognition of the nature of chronic mental health – and much less insight into what could be done to treat it – Frederick's condition went unchecked, although it was clear that his family recognised the difficulties he was having.

On the basis of our modern understanding, Frederick is likely to have been diagnosed as suffering from schizophrenia, a common, but chronic

A photograph of Orford Hill, Norwich. James Robinson's chemist's shop, where Frederick Page worked in 1873, can just be seen on the right. (Image courtesy of Norfolk County Council Library and Information Service)

mental health condition that causes a range of different psychologi-cal symptoms. This can include delusions – believing in things that are untrue – and hallucinations. In some cases, it can manifest itself in a form of psychosis where the sufferer is unable to distinguish between reality and imagination. In a rare number of situations it can also lead to acts of violence alongside the periodic episodes of dysfunction and disorder.

While living and working in Colchester, it had become Frederick's custom to catch the mail train to Manningtree each Saturday evening. He would then walk the mile or so from the station to Brantham to stay over at his parent's house and spend time with his family and friends, before returning on a Monday morning by the same route. During this time, he had become closely acquainted with Fanny Pleasant Clarke, a twenty-four-year-old domestic servant who worked for the family of William Green at Church House Farm in the village. Most often they would meet at the home of David Wheeler, his father's shepherd, whose wife Susannah had struck up a friendship with Fanny.

Fanny was a bright and attractive girl who had worked for the Greens for some four years. She was considered by William Green to be a respecta-ble, reliable and trustworthy employee. Her family lived in Little Stonham, about 20 miles north of Brantham, and she was one of five children born to parents Noah and Elizabeth Clarke.

The intimacy of the two youngsters had not gone unnoticed in the tight-knit community, where gossip was a frequent and staple currency of exchange. From September 1874, the pair had begun to write to each other throughout the week, making clear their affections. At one point Frederick had even hinted at marriage. But from the summer of the fol-lowing year, the relationship had started to cool when it became known that Fanny had been attracting the attentions of another admirer in Earl Stonham and Frederick's older brother, Robert Page, had been seen walk-ing out with Fanny and corresponding secretly with her. That she clearly preferred the attentions of the older sibling only added to Frederick's growing sense of jealousy and betrayal.

Matters came to a head on the evening of Sunday, 8 August 1875, when Fanny had arranged to meet Robert in a lane close to Braham Hall Farm. While the couple were walking together, Frederick jumped out from a nearby gate and accosted the pair. Angrily, he began to hurl insults at Fanny and pointedly asked for his letters to her to be given back to him. She replied that he could have them if he followed her back to Church House Farm. He then began to insinuate that she had been having a sexual relationship with her admirer in Earl Stonham. When she arrived back at Church House Farm that evening, Fanny was in tears and fainted before Mary Ann Smith, the wife of one of William Green's farm labourers.

The deep resentment that Frederick now felt was evident in his next communication with Fanny. On the Monday, while lodged back at No.29 South Street in Colchester, he wrote to her. The letter read simply:

> Will Miss F. Clarke inform Mr F. E. Page by return of post if it is convenient for her to meet him on Sunday evening next.

Having taken delivery of this curt missive, Fanny posted back to Frederick the thirty letters she had received from him since the start of their relationship. His subsequent reply, sent on the Thursday of that week, gave every impression of being a little more conciliatory:

> Dear Miss Clarke, - Thanks for my letters this morning. You have not replied to my letter, which, undoubtedly, you received yesterday. I regret having used those words, but I felt awfully wild. And to part friendly I ask you to meet me on Sunday evening next for I particularly want to see you. I await your reply by return of post.
> Yours truly,
> (signed) F.E. Page

While Fanny's reply was never discovered, it is known that she had acceded to his request and agreed to meet Frederick on Sunday 15 August. And despite the tone of his letter, it was clear that the jilted lover had already conceived the notion to murder Fanny that coming weekend. Two days before, during his lunch break, Frederick had gone into the shop of gunsmith John Boreham on the High Street in Colchester and purchased a six-barrelled revolver in a case along with a box of fifty Eley cartridges. Returning to work he was only too happy to show off the new weapon to fellow employee George Isom, claiming that he needed it for protection on his lonely Saturday evening walks from Manningtree railway station to Braham Hall Farm.

On the Sunday itself, Fanny had attended church for most of the day before visiting her friend Susannah Green. At about 6 p.m. that evening she left the Green's house, walking off in the direction of East Bergholt to meet Frederick Page. The pair were seen together by a number of local people from 7 p.m. onwards. And while it remained unclear what had transpired between them during those fateful two hours, a number of shots were heard in rapid succession just after 9 p.m. Frederick Page had apparently followed through with his plan to murder his sweetheart. Having used the revolver, he left Fanny for dead in Cross Road and headed for home still carrying the firearm.

When he arrived back at Braham Hall Farm, Frederick was questioned by his mother and father, who guessed that something untoward had happened. They found their son in a state of some agitation and acting very oddly. Initially he refused to say what had happened. A little later, he had a conversation with his brother Robert in the bedroom that they shared. When pressed about what he had done, Frederick finally confessed and pointed to the revolver case which lay on a window sill. Robert pocketed the weapon and alerted his father. Henry Page then left the house with his teenage son Horace and walked the route to Cross Road. Having seen a number of bloodstains in the lane, he realised that his son had indeed committed a serious crime.

Incredibly, despite being shot in the head a number of times at close range, Fanny Clarke did not die immediately. She managed to pick herself up from where she had fallen in the lane and at 9.10 p.m. staggered down the path towards Church House Farm. Samuel Smith, a yardman for William Green, had been standing in the doorway of the farmhouse as Fanny approached and watched incredulously as the domestic servant stumbled in, without a word, and sat down on a chair just inside the kitchen door. She was still wearing a white straw hat and her face and the front of her dress were covered in blood from what appeared to be a wound on her head. Smith called immediately for his employer and when William Green entered the kitchen he asked the yardman to go and fetch the local doctor. A short while later Green retrieved a letter that was sticking out of Fanny's pocket and handed it to his wife. It was a letter from Robert Page which apparently implicated Frederick in the crime that had occurred that evening. The Greens posted the correspondence off to the local constabulary.

Frederick Holman, a medical assistant, arrived sometime after 10.30 p.m. that evening and examined the patient. She was being looked after by Mrs Green and two women from the village. She had not moved from the chair in the kitchen and lay unconscious. Her arms were tightly folded in front of her and her hands were stained with blood. The blood on her head and neck was completely coagulated. While washing and sponging the young woman's face, Holman saw three head wounds. One, about an inch above the lobe of the left ear, was still bleeding freely.

He also observed two others over the middle of the right eyebrow. Two of these wounds had penetrated down to the bone of the skull. Holman stopped the bleeding from Fanny's head and bandaged the wounds as best he could. He then assisted Mrs Green in moving the young woman upstairs to her bed.

On the Monday morning, responding to the letter he had received overnight from William Green, Inspector William Clarke (apparently no relation of the victim) went to Braham Hall Farm to arrest Frederick Page. He explained that the letter found in Fanny Clarke's pocket the previous night had mentioned him and as a consequence of what was written, the police officer had reason to believe that Frederick knew something of the assault. The wine merchant's clerk did not deny being with Fanny on the Sunday, but refused to give an account of what had occurred. Inspector Clarke had no option but to arrest him. He was taken to the police station in Ipswich and charged with wounding with intent to do grievous bodily harm. He appeared briefly before local magistrates on the Tuesday morning before being remanded for a week pending further enquiries by the police.

Fanny Clarke remained seriously ill for three days, before finally passing away at 9.20 p.m. on the evening of Wednesday, 18 August. The next morning, Inspector Clarke revisited Braham Hall Farm, searching Frederick's bedroom for evidence in what was now a murder enquiry. Mr and Mrs Page directed him towards a box which contained a black coat and waistcoat, both of which appeared to be stained with spots of blood. A shirt bearing the label 'F.E.P.4.' and a number of white handkerchiefs were removed from a basket of dirty linen. They too looked to have traces of blood on them. An examination of the lane where it was believed the shooting had taken place also revealed a large pool of blood.

The coroner's inquest opened later that day at the Bull Inn, Brantham. The jury were taken to view the body of Fanny Clarke, which was still at Church House Farm. Having taken evidence on the identity of the deceased, the coroner, W.B. Ross, adjourned the proceedings pending the outcome of the post-mortem examination. This was carried out by Mr Manning the local doctor, assisted by J.W. Cook, a surgeon from Manningtree. The post-mortem showed that the injuries to the head had caused the death and were the result of five bullet-holes and not the effect of puncture wounds as had been suspected initially. Two bullets were found to be still lodged in the brain of the deceased while some bruising on other parts of the woman's body suggested either that she had received further blows to the body or had sustained the injuries while falling to the ground.

The Bull Inn, Brantham, where the Coroner's Inquest into the death of Fanny Pleasant Clarke was held in August 1875.

When the coroner's inquest resumed on Saturday, 21 August, it heard the results of Dr Manning's post-mortem, testimony from the police on the evidence found at Braham Hall Farm and various accounts of what had happened on the day of the shooting. The most telling of these were the statements given by Henry Page and his son Robert – both indicating clearly that Frederick had been the guilty party. It was also disclosed that the letter from Robert – found in the pocket of the injured woman – had been passed to Fanny by David Wheeler, the shepherd, during the after-noon before she had been assaulted. The letter had urged Fanny to see Frederick and break off her engagement with him. Most significantly, the murder weapon was handed over to the coroner by Robert Page. Having heard all of the evidence presented to them, the jury returned a verdict of 'wilful murder' against Frederick Page and he was then committed on a warrant from the coroner to face trial at the next assizes.

The body of Fanny Clarke was also buried the same day in the church-yard of St Mary's in Little Stonham. The mourners included her parents, sister and three brothers. In a morning service held the next day by the rector, the Revd J. Castley, worshipers were reminded that Fanny had been a

St Mary's Church in Little Stonham, where Fanny Clarke was buried on Saturday, 21 August 1875.

regular churchgoer and in an ironic twist of fate the date of her murder had been the anniversary of her first communion in the church six years before.

Frederick Page remained incarcerated in the Suffolk County Prison in Ipswich in the days following the inquest. He was brought again before the local magistrates on Tuesday, 24 August, in a hearing which continued the following day. Public interest in the case was running high and large crowds assembled outside the County Hall building on both days, with every seat in the large courtroom being taken by the eager spectators. Frederick maintained a sullen demeanour throughout the proceedings.

The evidence was, in the main, a repetition of that given at the inquest. Various witnesses testified to seeing Frederick and Fanny together during the early evening of Sunday, 15 August. The defence team, led by Mr

F.B. Philbrick, could do little to counter the weight of evidence presented against their client. In fact, the inquiry was punctuated by frequent objections and legal arguments about some of the questions put to witnesses by the prosecution – all of which seemed like a desperate attempt to prevent some of the more damning testimony against Frederick being disclosed ahead of the inevitable county court trial. When the proceedings ended around 6 p.m. on the second day, the prisoner was formally committed to stand trial on the charge of 'wilful murder'.

In the four-and-a-half months following the magisterial inquiry, Frederick Page continued to be held in the County Prison awaiting trial. His mental health had deteriorated such that he had become very violent and repeatedly threatened to kill those around him. Alongside this, he was both delusional and suicidal. In the final four weeks of his incarceration he was watched over night and day by the warders, who feared for his safety. In the end, he was certified insane by Dr Bartlett, the Medical Officer of the prison, and removed to Broadmoor Criminal Lunatic Asylum in Berkshire on Tuesday, 11 January 1876.

The following day he wrote his first letter home to his parents. It spoke clearly of his mental state:

My dear parents, - I thought you might be glad to hear I have arrived at this idiotic place all right. I cannot understand the reasons I am sent here, but I am told it is because I am insane, but I know I am not, and I shall

ASYLUM FOR CRIMINAL LUNATICS, BROADMOOR, SANDHURST, BERKSHIRE.

An engraving of Broadmoor Criminal Lunatic Asylum in 1867. (Wellcome Library, London)

write to the Ipswich magistrates and request an explanation. Everybody is very kind to me…I suppose I have to wait the Queen's pleasure, but I hope it won't please her long to keep me here…Everybody will think I am a big coward and afraid to be hung. But I shall write again & explain it to some of them…

The view of the doctors at the asylum was that while Frederick continued to have a perfect recollection of the facts connected to his crime – and was capable of understanding the nature of a criminal trial – he remained 'a person of defective and ill-balanced mind.' As such, despite a flurry of correspondence in the lead up to the opening of the Suffolk County Assizes in the early part of April 1876, the medical officers remained convinced that their patient was unable to stand trial. He was therefore to remain at Broadmoor until such a time as he was declared fit to answer the charges against him. In the event, that day never came.

Frederick continued to be housed at Broadmoor for the next ten years. He corresponded regularly with his family back in Suffolk and received occasional visits from them. His letters home suggest that he felt generally well cared for, although he appeared to resent any psychiatric interrogations concerning the nature of his crime. In later years he began to gripe about the food served in the institution and appeared to suffer from periodic episodes of poor physical health, which concerned his mother in particular. He also had occasional run-ins and confrontations with fellow inmates and asylum staff, much of which appeared to stem from his continuing delusions and insecurities.

By the summer of 1886, it was clear that Frederick's declining physical health was becoming a source of some concern to the doctors at Broadmoor. On 5 August, Dr Nicholson wrote to Mary Page to ask if she wished to visit her son, explaining that his patient was getting progressively weaker as an irritable complaint of the stomach was preventing him from retaining food. When Henry and Mary Page visited three days later, they found their son gravely ill. He eventually died in Broadmoor at 2.50 a.m. on Saturday, 28 August 1886. The coroner's inquest, conducted two days later, concluded that the death had been the result of a chronic inflammation of the stomach and bowels.

Frederick Ernest Page was buried in the private cemetery at Broadmoor. It was a measure of the continuing public interest in the nature of his crime that accounts of the murderer's demise appeared in provincial newspapers the length and breadth of the country. While largely overlooked now, the case is occasionally remembered locally as 'the sweetheart murder.'

4

THE JUNCTION PASSAGE DEBACLE

Lowestoft, 1913

Violence in the home is nothing new, and today much is known about the nature, extent and effects of domestic abuse. Current statistics show that one in four women – and any children in their care – experience domestic abuse at some point in their lives. This accounts for a quarter of all violent crime recorded in England.

In the Edwardian era, there was little such understanding of the pernicious nature of violence in the home and few measures available to prevent or tackle the widespread incidence of domestic abuse. While there had been some legislative responses to the problems faced by married women – including the Divorce and Matrimonial Causes Acts of 1857 and 1878 and the Married Women's Property Acts of 1870, 1882 and 1893 – the only real measure of protection afforded women came with the introduction of the Summary Jurisdiction (Married Women) Act of 1895, which gave magistrates the power to grant separation orders to wives driven from their homes by spousal abuse.

It was while seeking the protection of the law under these provisions that Fanny Chadd Thain was to experience the worst of her husband's abusive tendencies. On Thursday, 10 July 1913, Louis Thain's long reign of marital cruelty came to an end in an explosion of violence on the streets of Lowestoft. It is a case that has stayed in the collective consciousness of the town ever since.

Fanny was a widow when she met Louis Thain in late 1905. Born in Southwold in 1864, she was one of eleven children raised by parents

Richard and Maria Lord. Her father was a Norfolk-born ship owner who later opened up a pork butcher's shop in Southwold. By the time she was sixteen, Fanny was working as an assistant in the shop gaining experience which would later prove invaluable in her career. At some point during the next ten years she made the move to London and by the time of the 1891 census was working as the manageress of a café at No. 52, The Strand.

The owner of the London café was a forty-eight-year-old, Swiss-born confectioner named Joseph Gianella. He was a widower and employed four other staff alongside Fanny, having started his business at an earlier site in Kilburn. Fanny was clearly attached to both the business and her employer, for in early 1898 she married Joseph, who was by then a man of considerable means. Their marriage was to last but a few short months, however, for in the latter part of the year the confectioner passed away.

With her husband's death, Fanny Gianella was left with a comfortable annual income, her own fully-furnished house and a valuable collection of jewellery. The only restriction on her otherwise comfortable situation was that were she to remarry, her private income would be reduced by one third. She continued living in London for a few years beyond Joseph's death – the 1901 census showing her address to be No.80 Arngask Road, Lewisham, where she was recorded as 'living on own means' in the large five-bedroomed terraced house. By the time she met Louis Thain, she had moved back to Suffolk and was residing at No.1 Mattishall Villa on London Road South in the Kirkley area of Lowestoft. Here she continued to live the life of a comfortable middle-class Edwardian lady, content to play down her modest upbringing and earlier retail career.

Louis Thain was born in Lowestoft in 1869 to parents William and Martha Thain. He was one of eight children and by the time of the 1881 census the family were residing at a dwelling in the town called Willow House – his father being listed as a 'basket maker'. While it is by no means clear what profession, if any, Louis Thain pursued after leaving home, he was throughout his life described simply as 'an artist'.

Thain was well aware of Fanny Gianella's financial situation when he first asked for her hand in marriage. From the outset he sought to deceive her, claiming as part of his courtship that he was a successful Lowestoft fish merchant and promising to contribute to the household expenses each week to offset her loss of income. The couple were eventually married on Tuesday, 20 March 1906 at the Lowestoft Registry Office.

For the first four months of the marriage, Thain duly contributed £1 each week to the household budget. But the goodwill did not last long. By July, the payments had ceased – with Fanny Thain supporting them both on her reduced annual income from that point on. Her husband,

A copy of the Thain's 1906 marriage certificate. Louis fallaciously describes himself as a 'Fish Merchant,' while Fanny understates her age by four years. (General Register Office)

it seemed, preferred socialising and drinking in bars to earning a living, and soon got into financial difficulties. Fanny stuck by him, subsidising his drinking, covering his debts and paying for all of his food and clothing.

This situation continued until October 1908, when Fanny decided to take on the running of a small hotel in Hillington, near King's Lynn in Norfolk. For his part, Louis promised to help out with the management of the new enterprise, although any enthusiasm he had for the task soon evaporated. Frustrated by the hard work and long hours, he was soon to be seen gallivanting around the Norfolk countryside by car or on horse-back, leaving his ever-dependable wife to run the establishment.

He showed no more commitment when Fanny was taken ill in the summer of 1910 and had to go into hospital for a period of nine weeks, during which time she underwent two major operations. On returning to the hotel she found that nothing had been done and the entire stock of bed-linen had disappeared. With the business firmly run into the ground, Fanny was forced to close the hotel. She had lost some £300 in the ill-fated venture.

The couple moved back to Lowestoft in October 1910 and rented a three-storey house at No.12 Cleveland Road. The tenancy was in Louis' name, although once again it was Fanny who took responsibility for all

The house on Cleveland Road, Lowestoft, which the Thain's moved into during
October 1910.

of the rent, rates and household expenses. Emily Rudd, a young domestic servant, was taken on to lodge with them and support the running of
the house. To the outside world, they were a well-respected couple with a
happy marriage. Behind closed doors, it was a very different scenario.

Louis Thain's treatment of his wife deteriorated with the move back
to Lowestoft. His drinking became more frequent and problematical. He
would return home intoxicated, cursing Fanny and regularly pulling her
out of bed in the early hours of the morning to subject her to physical
abuse. He would punch her on the shoulder or chest and on one occasion
attempted to throw a piece of wood at her.

Having Emily Rudd as a lodger also brought with it further domestic
grief and a period of unwelcome public scrutiny. She had previously
worked for a Mrs Bunting, landlady of The Bushel public house in
Grimston, Norfolk (a couple of miles from the Hillington hotel). While
Fanny was happy with Rudd's service, it was clear that she knew little

about the servant's private life. She had noticed just before the Christmas of 1910 that the young girl appeared to be putting on weight and when she mentioned this, Rudd had made light of the situation, exclaiming: 'I am always stout, it is the good living.'

On the morning of Tuesday, 17 January 1911, Fanny had seen Rudd emerging from the water closet outside the house. The servant explained that she was not feeling well and Fanny advised her to go to bed, taking her up a cup of tea some twenty minutes later. While Rudd was in bed, Fanny noticed that there was blood on the floor of the water closet and also outside on the concrete path leading to the coal shed. When she later questioned Rudd about the matter, the servant replied, 'If you look in the coal shed you will know.'

Having looked into the coal shed just before midday, Fanny feared the worst and sent word to Louis to return home immediately. It was clear that Rudd had given birth to a child, which now lay dead at the back of their house. When Louis returned home at around 1.30 p.m. he was instructed by Fanny to look in the coal shed. On entering, he found the lifeless body of a baby boy, wrapped in a sack and lying in a disused coal-chute. He immediately called for a doctor and the police.

The inquest into the death was concluded within a month, with both Louis and Fanny being called to give evidence. Emily Rudd was taken from the house and accommodated within the Oulton Workhouse. It emerged during the proceedings that she had previously given birth to a young girl, who had died after eighteen months. The case attracted some attention in the local press, the *Lowestoft Journal* describing it as a 'Shocking Affair at Lowestoft.'

At the conclusion of the coroner's inquest, the jury found that there was insufficient evidence to warrant a verdict of manslaughter against Emily Rudd but considered her to be guilty of neglect in relation to the birth of the child. In addressing the servant girl, the East Suffolk coroner, Mr L.H. Vulliamy, announced that he entirely endorsed the verdict and said that Rudd had had a narrow escape from a verdict which might have had more serious consequences. He expressed the hope that the episode would serve as a lesson to her for the future.

Interestingly, throughout all of the inquiry, no one had sought to question who the father of the dead child might have been. It had been established that Emily Rudd had been taken on, without references, by Louis Thain, apparently on the recommendation of Mrs Bunting. Fanny had not even seen the girl until she arrived at Cleveland Road in the early part of October 1910. At the inquest, she admitted: 'We took her rather in a hurry.' We may never know whether there was more to this saga than emerged at the time, but Louis Thain's subsequent behaviour served only to confirm that he clearly had little regard for anyone other than himself.

The ill-treatment of Fanny Thain continued in the two years after Emily Rudd left, by which time the local police were being called on a regular basis to quell the disturbances at No.12 Cleveland Road. In January 1913, Fanny had taken in a lodger, who occupied two rooms of the house. Frederick William Davis was a travelling salesman who liked to play the piano. It was clear that Louis Thain had no liking for the man or his musical inclinations. As well as insinuating that Davis was conducting a secret affair with his wife, Thain made a commotion during one of Davis' recitals, prompting the salesman to complain to Fanny. When asked to explain his behaviour towards Davis, Louis swore at Fanny and became aggressive, threatening both her and the lodger with violence.

On Easter Sunday, 23 March, the abuse continued. Thain had asked for some money to enable him to entertain some friends for a day on the Norfolk Broads. When Fanny refused to oblige, he picked up a dinner knife and threatened her with it before throwing a vase. The vase hit her, causing her to fall back against a cabinet, bruising her hip and leaving her badly shaken. From that point on she refused to share a bedroom with her husband.

The Thain's domestic situation reached boiling point on 10 June 1913, made altogether worse by the fact that Fanny was also then grieving for her recently deceased sister. Following another confrontation, Fanny took an unloaded revolver that had belonged to her first husband and threatened to kill both herself and Louis. He ran terrified into another room, locking himself in, breaking a window and shouting into the street that his wife intended to kill him. For Frederick Davis, it was the final straw and he left his lodgings a few hours later.

The following day, Louis had the temerity to call at Lowestoft police station to report the incident with the revolver. When he returned home and explained what he had done, Fanny wasted no time in paying a visit to the station herself and setting the record straight, reiterating the catalogue of abuse she had experienced at the hands of her husband. She also asked for police protection.

Responding to her request, Sergeant Borley paid a visit to Cleveland Road later that day. He found Mrs Thain having tea with two close friends, a Mrs Bewley and her daughter Ethel. Not long after his arrival, Louis Thain returned home, worse for wear and brandishing a beer bottle. Ignoring the bemused Sergeant Borley, Thain proceeded to pick a fight with his wife – arguing over the position of the window blinds in the room – before throwing his beer bottle out into the street. At this point Borley intervened and succeeded in pacifying Thain enough to get him to leave the house.

The trouble then continued when Thain met another police officer in the vicinity of Cleveland Road. Superintendent John Page had been anticipating trouble and knew the history of domestic turmoil in the household. He agreed to accompany Louis back home in an ultimately misguided attempt to patch things up between the couple. Louis Thain responded by throwing a second beer bottle, this time catching Fanny on the cheek. He was given no option but to leave the house and sleep elsewhere – the Bewleys agreeing to stay overnight to support their friend.

Three days later and Fanny was confronted by another of her husband's transgressions. She had earlier lent him a valuable diamond ring, which she now realised he had pawned to support his drinking and carousing. With some embarrassment she was forced to redeem the ring from the pawnbrokers at the considerable cost of £6 8s. At this point she finally determined to end her marriage.

As if to confirm that she had taken the right course of action, Fanny then discovered on 28 June that another of her expensive rings was missing. The diamond Gypsy ring had been kept in a locked draw, which had been forced open. She contacted the police, who followed up the complaint. Sergeant Borley was able to retrieve the ring from Louis Thain before he could dispose of it. Fanny left the house after this to stay with the Bewleys at No.170 Denmark Road.

With the move from Cleveland Road, Fanny took advice on ending her marriage. She visited the offices of the solicitors Watson & Everitt and began to instigate proceedings for a judicial separation on the grounds of Louis' persistent cruelty. It took just a few days for her application to be acknowledged and a date to be set for the magistrates to hear the case. In the meantime, Louis Thain was frequently to be found loitering in the area of Denmark Road, rattling the windows of his wife's temporary home and trying to force an entry.

The date of the hearing was finally set for Thursday, 3 July. In the event, the case was adjourned immediately for one week to enable all of the witnesses to attend. Behind the scenes there had been some frantic negotiations to try and reach an amicable settlement without a prolonged legal battle. Fanny had made it quite clear that she simply wanted a separation and no order for payment. Louis Thain's behaviour had already given one firm of solicitors sufficient concern for them to write to Watson & Everitt saying that they were no longer prepared to represent him.

The adjourned hearing at the Lowestoft Magistrates Court resumed on Thursday, 10 July as planned. The Mayor and Chairman of the Bench was

The house on Denmark Road, Lowestoft, which was owned by a Mrs Bewley. Fanny Chadd Thain moved in with her during June 1913, having tired of Louis Thain's domestic abuse.

Mr F.T. Dewing. Fanny Thain had arrived in the company of Mrs Bewley and her daughter a short while before the proceedings commenced at 10 a.m., only to learn that the case would be heard after other items on the court agenda. Also present as witnesses were Superintendent Page, Sergeant Borley, some neighbours from Cleveland Road and the former lodger Frederick Davis. Conspicuous by his absence was Louis Thain.

When the case was called at 11 a.m., the errant husband was still not present and after various discussions between the magistrates, court clerk and solicitors, the hearing began without him. Mrs Thain recounted the history of her disastrous marriage to Louis and the frequent incidents of domestic abuse she had experienced at his hands. She ended by saying how afraid and alone she had felt before leaving Cleveland Road and confirmed that she had feared Louis would do her harm. It was a telling and prophetic moment.

Fanny could not have known at this point that Louis was indeed planning to do her harm. Early on the morning of the hearing, he had left his

Old Nelson Street, Lowestoft, where Louis Thain was living prior to his divorce hearing. (Lowestoft Heritage Workshop Centre)

lodgings at No.35 Old Nelson Street and had asked a friend to drive him over to Great Yarmouth, where he had gone into a post office to obtain a gun licence. Passing himself off as William Machin, he had given his address as 'Offendene', Christchurch Road, Norwich and had then been given the required licence. With this in hand he had purchased a suitable revolver and ammunition from a local gunsmith.

To the modern observer, it seems remarkable that a gun could be purchased so easily, but until 1920 there were no effective controls on the ownership of firearms. The Pistols Act of 1903 had placed some restrictions on the purchase of small handguns by individuals who were not householders, but those with property did not even require a licence. They had only to provide reasonable evidence that they planned to use the pistol on their own property. By applying for a gun or game licence the purchaser could effectively obtain a gun, without this need for further evidence, and be within the law by carrying it around with them. The introduction of the Firearms Act of 1920 made it illegal to possess a weapon without first obtaining a certificate from the police and registering each individual firearm, although local forces could only deny someone a licence if they believed the applicant to be 'unfitted to be trusted with a firearm.'

Before leaving the post office, Thain had also sent a telegram to his wife, purportedly from her brother George. The message asked Fanny to meet him off the train at Lowestoft railway station at 10 a.m. It was clear from this that Thain had planned to lure his wife to the station, where he would be armed with the handgun. Fanny had received the telegram before setting off for the courtroom that morning and did in fact walk down to the station around 10 a.m., having learnt that her case was not to be heard immediately. Fortunately for her, when all of the train's passengers had disembarked and it was clear that George was not among them, Louis Thain was nowhere to be seen. He had given up waiting and had disappeared into the town in pursuit of another drink.

Following Fanny's appearance before the magistrates, Superintendent Page was called to give evidence. He outlined the incidents that had involved the police from the morning of 11 June, when Louis Thain had first reported his wife for brandishing a revolver. The officer then explained that he had agreed to provide some police protection for Mrs Thain in the interests of both parties and deposed that since she had moved to the Denmark Road address, the police had been providing protection on a nightly basis.

It was at this stage in the proceedings that Louis Thain entered the courtroom, dressed in a light-coloured suit and straw hat, and visibly the worse for drink. As he pushed past the court usher, he was challenged by the magistrates' clerk about why he had not been present at the start of the hearing. Thain apologised and explained that he had been to Great Yarmouth to get extra witnesses. He was rebuked by the clerk but allowed to take a seat just as Mrs Bewley prepared to give evidence.

Mrs Bewley corroborated Superintendent Page's version of events on 11 June and told the court of Thain's unruly behaviour in the weeks prior to the hearing. She and her daughter had stayed with Mrs Thain every night until her friend had moved in with them. While listening to this, Louis Thain interrupted occasionally and was admonished a number of times. Yet when asked at the end of the testimony whether he wished to question the witness, he declined.

As the last witness called in support of Fanny Thain, Sergeant Borley was able to outline in some detail the various events at Cleveland Road and the damage Louis Thain was alleged to have caused to the Bewley's home in Denmark Road. At the end of this, Thain again declined to ask any questions and was then invited to call his own witnesses.

What followed was a largely inadequate attempt to refute the earlier testimony. A string of witnesses, including various neighbours and Alice Rose – a former day servant that the Thains had employed after Emily Rudd had left them – testified that in their view the couple had been happily married and they had seen no evidence of Mrs Thain's ill-treatment.

Rose even went on to suggest that it was Fanny Thain who had the drink problem, testifying that she had often been asked to buy whisky for her former employer and had seen her drink it.

When he entered the witness box, Louis Thain continued in this vein, stating that his wife's drinking had been at the root of their marital problems. He also hinted at her relationship with Frederick Davis, the music-loving lodger, but under cross-examination would not be drawn to say that it amounted to an affair. The magistrates seemed unimpressed with his assertion that he had often been forced to sleep on the floor of the kitchen during the frequent arguments with his wife. And when Nelson Wyles, Mrs Thain's solicitor, questioned him about his own drinking, Louis gave an unconvincing performance in stating that while he was no teetotaller, he had never been the worse for drink. All of this had done little to support his case and he did himself no further favours as he took umbrage when asked if he had worked prior to October 1912.

When Mr Wyles suggested calling both Frederick Davis and the land-lord of a local public house to rebut the suggestions about Fanny Thain's 'affair' and her secret whisky-drinking, the bench announced that this was unnecessary. They had already heard enough, and having retired for just a few minutes to consider their verdict, the Mayor then announced their decision – they had decided to grant the application for a separation order with costs of £2 3s against the defendant.

Fanny Thain and her friends looked relieved and contented. Mr Wyles thanked Superintendent Page for the conduct of his officers towards Mrs Thain, but Page was quick to point out that it was not only a case of pro-tecting her, but of preventing Mr Thain from committing an offence. The words must have come back to haunt him later.

Louis Thain left the Magistrates Court on Regent Road quietly and quickly, heading briskly along London Road North before turning onto Denmark Road. A little way along the street he entered Junction Passage, a small alleyway which ran north onto Tonning Street.

In the meantime, Fanny Thain had left the court building in the company of her friends the Bewleys and Frederick Davis, who was accom-panying the women fearing further trouble. His hunch was not to be ill-founded. They headed off along Regent Street in the opposite direction, turning into Alexandra Road and then joining Clapham Road, which took them down to Tonning Street.

As the quartet entered the Tonning Street end of Junction Passage, Louis stepped forward and surprised them all by shouting, 'Ah, now I've got you all together.' The two Bewley women stood bravely in front of their friend to protect her, but Louis Thain became wildly animated in trying

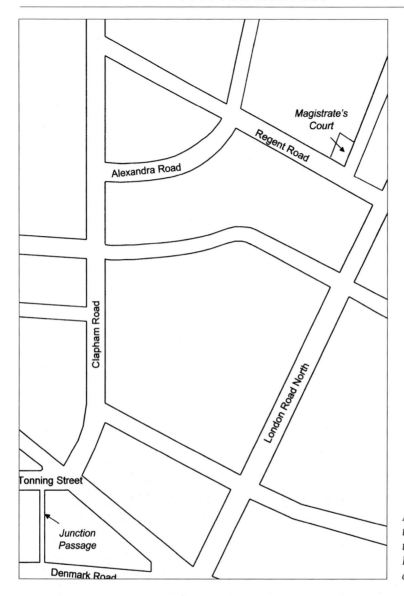

A map showing the two routes taken towards Junction Passage on the day of the shootings.

to speak to his wife. To everyone's horror he then produced the revolver from his jacket pocket and without hesitation pointed it in the direction of Mrs Bewley and fired. As he did so, Miss Ethel Bewley ran forward and the bullet hit her in the back of the head. She collapsed onto the ground.

Frederick Davis pulled Fanny Thain further along the alleyway in a vain attempt to escape onto Denmark Road, but Louis was quick to catch them up and as they reached the property at No. 2 Junction Passage, Fanny screamed and fell near the fence of the cottage. Louis fired the gun twice, hitting her in the face, and leaving her for dead. Davis, now in fear

A photograph showing the entrance to Junction Passage from Denmark Road – the route taken by Louis Thain. The picture was taken in the early 1970s before the houses in the area were demolished to make way for a new road. (Lowestoft Heritage Workshop Centre)

The entrance to Junction Passage from Tonning Street taken by Fanny Thain and her friends. (Lowestoft Heritage Workshop Centre)

for his own life, continued to run, with Thain bearing down on him and still firing.

Another man now entered the drama. Arthur George Myhill, a forty-eight-year-old fisherman, had emerged from No.2 Junction Passage having heard all of the commotion while finishing his dinner. He set off in pursuit of Thain, who then attempted to shoot himself in the head while still running along the alleyway. The gun failed to go off.

The runners now spilled onto Denmark Road, watched by countless spectators who had come out from their homes and business premises to see what was happening. Myhill caught hold of Thain's shoulder and began to wrestle with him, but Thain shook himself free, shouting, 'Don't interfere with me or I'll shoot you.' He then raised his arm and shot Myhill directly in the mouth. The fisherman ran but a few yards before collapsing and rolling on the ground, mortally wounded. Thain then put the revolver to the right side of his own head and fired. His body slumped in the roadway.

Midway down Junction Passage. The home of Arthur Myhill is on the left. (Lowestoft Heritage Workshop Centre)

Some of the key players in the drama: Louis Thain (left); Elizabeth Myhill (top); Arthur George Myhill (bottom); and Fanny Thain (right). (Lowestoft Heritage Workshop Centre)

Henry Pemberton, a greengrocer, had witnessed almost the entire sequence of events and ran across just after this to remove the revolver from Louis Thain as he lay dying in the street. He was then joined by PC Rowe and Dr Augustus Marshall. A passing cab was waived down and the doctor accompanied the injured Thain to the town hospital. A short while later the police ambulance arrived and PC Rowe had the unenviable task of taking the dead body of Arthur Myhill to the mortuary.

Elizabeth Myhill had no idea at this stage that her husband had been killed in the pursuit. She was busy attending to the injured Mrs Thain who still lay against her fence in Junction Passage. Further along the alleyway, passers-by were assisting the wounded and unconscious Ethel Bewley and her distraught mother.

Louis Thain's short but violent attack had brought death and injury to the normally quiet streets of the Suffolk fishing town. In the aftermath of the debacle, Arthur Myhill had died almost instantly. Louis himself was still breathing when he reached hospital but died later that afternoon. Miss Ethel Bewley was treated at the Clapham Hotel before being taken home to Denmark Road. While the bullet that hit her had entered her skull and part of her brain had protruded from the wound, she had regained consciousness later that evening and went on to survive the attack. Frederick Davis had been hit in the shoulder by a bullet which, while leaving a hole in his coat, had failed to penetrate his skin. Fanny Thain, the long-suffering wife, had also been shot in the back of the head and had sustained injuries to her nose and mouth in the fall. However, she too would go on to survive the assault.

A contemporary photograph of the Junction Passage crime scene. (Lowestoft Heritage Workshop Centre)

87

The inquest into the deaths opened that same evening before Mr L.H. Vulliamy, in the courtroom which had earlier seen Louis Thain testifying against his wife. The coroner announced to the jury that as there was little information about the events leading to the deaths, the proceedings would concentrate only on confirming the identity of the two deceased men. Superintendent Page identified the body of Thain while grief-stricken widow Elizabeth Myhill confirmed the identity of her husband. The coroner then adjourned the inquest until 3.30 p.m. on the following Monday.

Louis Thain's body was laid to rest in Lowestoft Cemetery on the morning of Saturday, 12 July 1913. The burial service was conducted in private, without the unwanted scrutiny of the press or public, and attended only by the undertaker, Horace Riches, his pall-bearers and the Revd Cadman, a curate from St Margaret's Church in the town.

Two days later the adjourned inquest resumed at the Police Court. It emerged that two of Thain's brothers had previously committed suicide, prompting some speculation as to the mental state of Louis Thain on the day of the shootings. The only other revelation to emerge occurred when the coroner produced four sheets of closely written notepaper which had been addressed to him and marked 'Private'. Thain had written the letter on 10 July, prior to the hearing of the magistrates, which suggested that he had always intended to take his own life. The coroner said that the early part of the letter contained a series of unfounded allegations which he was not prepared to make public. The rest of the missive left instructions about how he wanted his possessions to be disposed of, including what should happen in the event that his wife predeceased him. The coroner said this could be taken to infer that Thain had also intended to kill his wife.

The outcome of the inquest was never in doubt. The jury took less than five minutes to reach a verdict of 'wilful murder by Thain' in the case of Arthur Myhill and 'felo-de-se' – feloniously committing suicide – in the case of Louis Thain.

Arthur Myhill was buried in heavy rain the following day at Lowestoft Cemetery before a large crowd of onlookers and not far from where

A contemporary photograph showing Arthur Myhill's house in Junction Passage (left) and the spot on Denmark Road where Louis Thain took his own life (right). (Lowestoft Heritage Workshop Centre)

Another photograph of Denmark Road taken around the time of the murder. (Lowestoft Heritage Workshop Centre)

Thain's service had taken place only three days earlier. The funeral was conducted by Mr S. Rowe, a missionary at the Fishermen's and Sailors' Bethel, who referred briefly to the courageous act which had cost Myhill his life. An appeal by the Mayor to raise funds to support the fisherman's widow eventually raised over £120 – a considerable amount of money at that time.

Fanny Thain had endured years of physical and mental abuse at the hands of a cruel and self-centred husband. That she had also survived the final desperate attempt on her life was nothing short of a miracle. But survive she did, later moving away from Lowestoft and eventually passing away in London in 1925, when she was sixty years old.

5

A MOTORMAN STANDS TRIAL

Ipswich, 1920

Within the annals of British crime history, there are an overwhelming number of murder stories that are little more than open and shut cases – criminal investigations and trials which leave us with few misgivings about the guilty party. The fictional murder mystery may continue to be an ever-popular public pre-occupation, but its counterpart in the world of true crime is a rare narrative indeed. That said, there are a small number of cases which, while appearing to be watertight in their investigative results and judicial outcomes, leave us with that irritating and unsettling element of doubt, especially where a public execution is concerned. Such is the case of Frederick William Storey.

Storey's trial for the murder of thirty-two-year-old housekeeper Sarah Jane Howard, in May 1920, was built on a comprehensive and compelling body of circumstantial evidence. Witnesses placed him near the crime scene on the night in question. Testimony indicated that the victim was well known to him. A convenient murder weapon was found at his home. And scientific analysis of his clothing revealed bloodstains apparently consistent with the crime committed. Having heard all of this evidence, the jury took just fifteen minutes to reach its verdict of 'Guilty' and the trial judge had no option but to pronounce the death penalty for the ill-fated Ipswich tram driver.

Of course modern forensic science could have addressed many of the lingering concerns about this case. But all the test tubes and DNA analysis in the world would not help to shed light on other, equally persistent, queries surrounding Storey's apparent guilt. As such, it is a case worthy of further attention.

It was in the early hours of Saturday, 7 February 1920 that the dead body of Sarah Howard was discovered near a wire fence along a quiet, private lane leading to Maidenhall Farm in Ipswich. Walter Hill, a foreman platelayer for the Great Eastern Railway, was busy at work checking a stretch of track from the Halifax Junction – on the main London to Norwich line – at around 8.50 a.m. He saw the body lying on the opposite side of the fence from the railway line and walked across to investigate.

The railwayman could see that the young woman was dead and made no attempt to touch the body. Her frost-covered corpse was rigid and lay face-down on its right side, against the bottom wire of the fence. She was fully-clothed except for a hat which rested close-by. Hill could see several ugly wounds on the woman's head and a considerable pool of blood beneath this on the ground. He shouted to a colleague who was working some way further down the track and instructed him to fetch the police. So began the official investigation.

Sergeant Hudson and PC Finch joined Walter Hill around 9.30 a.m. Hudson had been patrolling on Wherstead Road, less than a mile away, when informed about the discovery and both officers reached the crime scene by taking the private track which ran from the side of Halifax Lodge to Maidenhall Farm. This was not a public right of way but was a route used regularly by farm workers and a number of families who had allotments on the Maidenhall Farm estate – a fact that would have some bearing later in the case.

Surveying the scene, Sergeant Hudson could see that foul play had been involved, but noted that there were no signs on the ground of any sort of struggle having taken place. He left PC Finch in charge and went off to telephone his senior officers. Within an hour Hudson was back at the scene accompanied by Superintendent Firman, Police Surgeon Stanley Hoyland and Detective Inspector Wood. The latter assumed responsibility for the subsequent investigation and the body was removed to the mortuary for a post-mortem examination by Dr Hoyland.

It took no time at all for the detectives to establish the identity of the murder victim. William John Kettle, a draughtsman and widower residing at No.133 Camden Road, had reported his housekeeper as missing on the Friday evening. He had given her name as Sarah Howard, explaining that he had seen her last at 7 p.m. and was concerned for her safety as she had rarely been out later than 9.30 p.m at night. Late on the Saturday morning he appeared once more at Ipswich police station, more than ever concerned about her whereabouts and enabling the police to con-

The house on Camden Road, Ipswich, where Sarah Jane Howard worked as a housekeeper to William John Kettle.

firm the identity of the body they had discovered earlier. Kettle was also able to provide the detectives with the name of a suspect in the murder enquiry.

The police acted promptly in following up the lead. They were told that before taking up her position as housekeeper to William Kettle, Howard had worked as a conductress for the Ipswich Corporation Tramways, joining the service in January 1918. During that time she had appar-

A Derby Road tramcar, as driven by Frederick William Storey. (Ipswich Transport Museum)

ently become acquainted with one of the corporation's tram drivers – a Frederick William Storey, known to all of his work colleagues as 'Fred'.

Having found out that Fred Storey was working that morning, DI Wood located him at midday driving a Derby Road tramcar. With Storey detained for questioning, the detective arranged for an immediate search of the driver's home at No.42 Gower Street. At 12.45 p.m. that afternoon, he arrived at the address with Sergeant Hudson and Dr Hoyland.

The search yielded what the investigators believed to be promising clues. Guided by Storey's twenty-one-year-old daughter, Myra Priscilla, they removed articles of clothing that she said her father had been wearing on the Friday evening. They also discovered a mackintosh, a pair of brown boots, the front of a shirt, a piece of newspaper and a small hammer – all appeared to show traces of blood, although the hammer was damp and looked as if it had been washed not long before. It was Dr Hoyland's contention that the bloodstains were recent and human.

With the discoveries at Gower Street, the police focused squarely on Fred Storey as the prime suspect in the murder investigation. The questioning of the tram driver began in earnest later that afternoon. He was cautioned and told that the dead body of a woman named Howard had been found in a field adjacent to Wherstead Road and was asked to give an account of his whereabouts on the Friday evening.

Storey began by mentioning a visit he had received on the Saturday morning from William Kettle. It later transpired that the draughtsman had gone to the Cornhill area of Ipswich at around 10 a.m. looking for a 'Mr Storey,' unaware that the body of his missing housekeeper had been found earlier that morning. Following some directions from a tram inspector, Kettle had located Fred Storey's tramcar some thirty minutes later and had climbed up on the footboard, where he began to challenge the bemused driver about Sarah Howard. Storey had not denied knowing the housekeeper, but told Kettle, 'I only know her to talk to.' When asked when he had last seen her, Storey had apparently told Kettle that he thought it was the previous Sunday night, 'up at Derby Road.' Kettle was unconvinced, adding, 'I think you know a good deal about her.' Storey replied simply, 'You have made a mistake old man. I know nothing about her.' It was after this that Kettle had called in at the police station to check if anything further was known about the whereabouts of his missing housekeeper.

Kettle had his reasons for seeking out Fred Storey, as we will discover, but as the tram driver relayed the incident to DI Wood that Saturday afternoon, it must have seemed an odd, if somewhat incriminating, episode to bring up when the police officer had merely asked Storey to explain where he had been on the Friday evening. In all likelihood, it must have added to Woods' already strong suspicion that they had indeed found the killer of Sarah Howard.

When he moved on to describe his whereabouts on the Friday evening, Storey gave a clear and comprehensive statement. He claimed to have finished work just after 6 p.m., going straight home for tea. He left at 7.55 p.m., walking first to the Cornhill, then to Croft Street and later as far as the Black Bridge on Wherstead Road. Later he had turned back and while walking close to Uncle Tom's Cabin (a public house) had met and conversed with two police constables, one of whom he knew as PC Snell. He had walked with the officers for some way in the direction of his home and had arrived back at No.42 Gower Street, where he found his daughter Myra and her friend Ivy Woollard in the living room. A little after 9 p.m. that evening he had left home a second time, on this occasion going straight to the Conservative Club in town, where he stayed until almost 11 p.m. A fellow tram driver, Bertram Wragg, had left the club with him and the two had walked together as far as Purfleet Street. Storey claimed to have gone straight home and to bed after this, rising on the Saturday morning to head into work around 7.30 a.m.

Having given this statement, Storey was then asked to describe what he had been wearing the previous evening when he left home. He replied, 'Cap, collar and tie, private jacket and waistcoat, and mackintosh.' DI Wood then interrogated him about the items found during the search of No.42 Gower Street. When shown some of the bloodstains, he replied, 'I don't know anything about them unless they came from my face. I cut it with a razor.' In support of this, Storey did at this time have a piece of sticking plaster on his left cheek. When Wood asked him to remove the clothes he was wearing for further examination, a small bloodstain was observed on the left cuff of the tram driver's woollen vest – again Storey claimed to know nothing about it.

The tram driver was kept in the police station overnight in the charge of DC Cobb. At one point he had an angry exchange with the officer, exclaiming:

I am blowed if this is all right. I suppose they think I did this? If I had done a murder last night, do you think I should have come on the cars this morning? Nobody has seen any difference in me. Do you see any difference in me?

Just after 1 p.m. on the Sunday afternoon, Storey was again cautioned and then formally charged with the murder. He immediately declared that he was 'Not guilty.' The items removed during the search of his home were despatched to Dr Bernard Henry Spilsbury, the honorary forensic pathologist to the Home Office, for further scientific analysis.

On the morning of Monday, 9 February, Storey appeared before the Ipswich Police Court and was remanded for a week on the charge of wilful murder. The courtroom was packed to capacity and a large crowd had gathered outside the building prior to his arrival. He faced the magistrates dressed in his tram service tunic and appeared downcast. The proceedings lasted only a short while, after which Storey was removed from the court and taken back to a police cell.

The coroner's inquest opened the same day at St Michael's Schoolroom on Upper Orwell Street. Dr Hoyland testified that during his preliminary examination of the body at the scene, he had discovered a total of eight wounds on the head of the deceased. One of these was a depressed fracture behind Sarah Howard's left ear which had converged into another wound, causing a hole in the skull some 2in long by an inch wide. He confirmed

Ipswich. Town Hall and Post Office. 11.

Ipswich Town Hall (right), which housed the main Ipswich police station in which Fred Storey was held during the murder investigation.

that the blows had been separately administered and could not have been self-inflicted. There was some bruising on the back of the right hand and a small cut, a quarter of an inch in length, on the wrist. Two similar wounds appeared on the left of Howard's face and there was also a small, inch-long cut in her left ear. Along with the slight blacking below her left eye, this suggested that the housekeeper had died trying to defend herself.

Asked his professional opinion, Dr Hoyland said that while some of the head wounds were superficial in nature, two were sufficient to have caused immediate death. The murder weapon was 'a blunt instrument' and at the time of the examination she had been dead 'ten or twelve hours or more.' He also confirmed that she had been pregnant.

In his testimony, William Kettle explained that he had advertised for a housekeeper in the late summer of 1919. He had received several letters in reply, including one from Sarah Howard, who was lodging at No.33 Beaconsfield Road in Ipswich. In a subsequent letter, she signed herself as

'Mrs Jane Howard.' She claimed to have been married, but said that her husband had died some time earlier. Kettle had engaged her and she took up the post and moved in on Saturday, 30 August. She brought with her a son, who was said at that time to be three-and-a-half years of age.

Asked if his housekeeper had performed her duties to his satisfaction, Kettle replied, 'Absolutely.' Then came the most significant revelation. He had noticed in the early part of the year that Howard appeared to be pregnant. When he asked her on 18 January what she planned to do about the situation, the housekeeper had apparently burst into tears, before confirming that she was expecting a baby in the first week of March.

Despite all of the concern he was keen to demonstrate after her disappearance, Kettle seemed to have shown little sympathy to Sarah Howard on learning the news of her pregnancy. He told her immediately that she should endeavour to find another home before the birth. It was his understanding that on the night of the murder she was continuing to do just that.

Kettle had also quizzed her about the father of the child and in his testimony said that Howard had given him 'the name of a man.' The coroner at once asked for clarification – 'She mentioned a name?' Kettle simply replied, 'Yes.' Incredibly, considering the significance of this disclosure, he was not pressed further on the matter. He continued his testimony by saying that he had never seen her in the company of any man and, until she had begun to look for alternative lodgings, had not been in the habit of going out late at night.

The inquest was adjourned until Friday, 13 February, to enable the police to conclude their investigations. From this point on DI Wood's team began to build a strong case against Fred Storey, although the nature of the evidence remained largely circumstantial. Herein lay the challenge for the authorities. For Storey to face the death penalty, a jury had to be convinced that he had not only murdered Sarah Howard, but that the evidence presented against him demonstrated his guilt beyond all reasonable doubt.

At the time of the murder Storey was forty-two years old. He had been born in Ipswich in September 1877 to parents Robert and Susannah Storey and was the youngest of five children. He had married his wife, Minnie Priscilla, sometime before 1901 and the couple had six children – a seventh child being born to the thirty-nine-year-old while Storey was imprisoned and awaiting trial for the murder.

Starting his working life as a labourer, Storey had joined the Ipswich Corporation Tramways as a track cleaner shortly after it had taken over the tram system operated by the previous Ipswich Tramway Company. By 1904, the tram network covered an area of over 10 miles, its single-track lines radiating out from the centre of Ipswich to most parts of the town, powered by overhead electric trolley wires. By 1920, the corporation's tramcars, with their distinctive green and cream liveries, were serving a population of 85,000 and carrying around 7½ million passengers a year.

Storey took to the work well and in January 1904 received the first of a number of promotions, his weekly pay rising to 18s. On 2 April 1905, this was further increased to 20s a week – a good wage by the standards of the day. In June 1907 he became a tram conductor and later a tram driver or 'motorman'. His tram service was broken only by his conscription into the Army during the First World War and by the time he returned home in June 1918 Storey had served in France, Belgium, Egypt and Salonika.

Returning to civilian life and his pre-war occupation, Storey found that many of the jobs on the Ipswich tramway had been filled during the war years by female workers. One of these was Sarah Howard, who worked as a conductress until March 1919, when she and others were laid off with the return of men from the Western Front. Storey never denied knowing Howard. A key question at both the coroner's inquest and the later murder trial was just how closely acquainted had they become?

When the coroner's inquest resumed on 13 February, some new information was revealed about the murder victim. The jury heard from James Seymour, a Fenland farmer from Witchford near the Isle of Ely. He was Howard's half-brother, and explained that Sarah had previously been a schoolteacher in the village. She had left the neighbourhood after having an illegitimate child some seven years earlier. While he had not seen her since that time, he said his wife had received occasional letters from her during the period. From the disclosures that followed, it was clear that the son referred to could not have been the same boy that was now lodged at William Kettle's – he was too young. It was later learnt that Howard had given birth to three children, one of which had been stillborn. The whereabouts of the seven-year-old was never made clear.

When William Kettle was recalled to give evidence, he outlined how he had tracked down Fred Storey on the Saturday morning and had asked him about his missing housekeeper. The draughtsman himself now faced some tough questioning – the jury challenging him about the answers he had given during the first session of the inquest and pointing out that he had not previously mentioned Storey by name. Kettle went on to say that after he had confronted Howard about being pregnant, she had confided in him that she had been seeing a man and had mentioned Storey's name a number of times after this.

Dr Hoyland was also recalled and gave further medical testimony based on the post-mortem examination he had carried out after the first hearing.

The autopsy had revealed more extensive damage to Sarah Howard's skull than he had previously observed. He now believed that she had received at least eleven blows to the head, but had not changed his opinion that the fracture of the skull had been the cause of death.

Hoyland also described how the clothes, mackintosh, boots, shirt front, newspaper and hammer had been found at Storey's home and showed traces of blood. He said that he believed the hammer could have caused the wounds he had already described. The inquest jury was then told by Superintendent Firman that the articles in question had been submitted to Dr Spilsbury for further analysis, but the earliest date that the forensic pathologist could attend the inquest was Friday, 27 February. The hearing was adjourned for two weeks to allow for his attendance on that day.

When the inquest resumed at the Town Hall, a succession of witnesses were called to give evidence not only of the alleged relationship between Storey and Howard, but also of the various sightings of the two on the night of the murder. Many of those testifying were employees of Ipswich Corporation Tramways and were well known to Fred Storey. The bulk of this evidence would be replayed later at the criminal trial.

The inquest proceedings were enlivened by the attendance of Dr Bernard Spilsbury of St Bartholomew's Hospital in London. Spilsbury was thirty-three years old, tall, good-looking and immaculately turned out. As a forensic pathologist, he was already a household name, having achieved early success in his career by giving evidence at the trial of poisoner Dr Hawley Harvey Crippen, who was found guilty of murdering his wife Cora in 1910. In 1915, Spilsbury's testimony was crucial in securing a conviction against lady-killer George Smith, infamous for the 'Brides in the Bath' murders. And within a couple of years of appearing in Ipswich, he would testify in yet another high-profile murder trial – that of Major 'Excuse Fingers' Armstrong, who was convicted of poisoning his wife with arsenic in 1922. Much later the 'Father of Forensics' would meet with an unfitting end himself, when, in 1947, aged seventy, he committed suicide, having never fully recovered from the wartime deaths of his beloved wife and two of his sons.

Dr Spilsbury testified that he had carried out an examination of the clothes sent to him by DI Wood. He found red stains, spots and smears on some of the clothing, the hammer and the newspaper. His tests thus far had revealed only that they were mammalian bloodstains – and some had been washed or diluted. He also said that the stains on the mackintosh were no older than two weeks from the date when he had examined them (11 February) and that he had yet to examine the newspaper in detail.

In essence, the testimony added little to what was already known about the forensic evidence.

The coroner's jury deliberated for three-quarters of an hour before the Foreman returned to announce that they found the death had been due to a fracture of the skull and laceration of the brain caused by blows from a blunt instrument, and that the blows had been inflicted by Frederick William Storey. The coroner asked whether he was returning a verdict of wilful murder, to which the Foreman replied, 'That is so.' Storey was committed for trial at the county assizes.

The murder trial began in Bury St Edmunds on Friday, 28 May 1920, before Mr Justice Darling. In addition to being a lawyer, Charles John Darling had been a Conservative politician and had served as a Member of Parliament for Deptford from 1888 to 1897. In that latter year, he had been appointed a Judge of the High Court of Justice and had become a member of the Privy Council in 1917. Mr C.F. Gill and Mr Travers Humphreys conducted the prosecution, while Mr A.S. Leighton – instructed by Mr Claude Marshall of Ipswich – defended.

At the opening of the proceedings, Fred Storey was called before the court. He stepped into the dock and in answer to the charge put to him, pleaded 'Not guilty' in a firm, clear voice.

Mr Gill then outlined the case for the prosecution. He explained how the dead body of Sarah Howard had been found on the morning of 7 February and described the key features of the murder. In particular, he pointed to the fact that the lonely nature of the murder scene suggested that this was a place selected specifically for the commission of the crime. In other words, the housekeeper must have been induced to go there by the man who took her life. He argued that Storey had been the man concerned and that he had lured Howard to her death in a pre-arranged meeting at about 8.30 p.m. that night. The victim had been pregnant and was looking for Storey to support her as the father of the child. Gill went on to suggest that Storey had demonstrated 'great self-possession' in walking part of the way to his home afterwards with a patrolling police officer. The prosecution further contended that the crime must have been committed between 8.30 p.m. and 9 p.m. on that fateful Friday.

While it is an obvious cliché to point out that the complexion of a trial like this would have been very different if the full resources of our present medical and forensic sciences had been available at the time, the fact remains that the commonplace nature of modern DNA-testing would, at the very least, have answered one of the questions central to the murder: was it Fred Storey's child that Sarah Howard was carrying?

In underpinning his case, Gill called a stream of witnesses to place Fred Storey near the murder scene on the night in question and to provide evidence of his sexual attachment to Sarah Howard. Sergeant Hudson, who had been called to the scene following Walter Hill's discovery of the body, testified that an allotment shed used by Storey lay only 520 yards from the spot where the murder occurred. This was certainly convenient evidence to support the notion that Storey had lured his lover to a spot well known to him. Perhaps it could be contended that the two had met there before, the shed providing them with a discrete place in which to conduct their illicit affair.

The problem with this line of reasoning is that it fails to fit neatly with the prosecution's assertion that the crime scene was a 'very lonely spot' chosen specifically for the purpose of murder. Fred Storey had grown up in the area and knew the geography of the estate only too well. While he may have chosen the spot for a romantic liaison, it is hard to imagine him choosing it as a preferred location for murder – it being so close to his allotment. Of course, it could be argued that he had not planned to kill at all, but had been driven to commit the crime in the heat of the moment – perhaps realising that Howard's emotional state and precarious domestic situation was about to place his infidelity under the uncomfortable spotlight of the public gaze.

Yet it was the prosecution's own interpretation that Storey had demonstrated 'great self-possession' in the aftermath of the alleged murder. Where then was this same composure in planning his route home? Faced with the choice between a quiet, private and unlit route through the farm estate and an exit along a well-lit public thoroughfare, it seems odd that our murderer would have selected the latter, especially if we are to believe that he was carrying the murder weapon and may have had traces of blood on his clothes. The same could be said of the journey to the scene earlier that evening. It would indeed take some confidence to plan to meet the woman you intended to murder by setting out on such a visible route – one that was patrolled by police officers known to you and which served as a main artery for the tram network on which your work colleagues drove along with such regularity.

Such questions serve only to highlight the difficulty of proving beyond reasonable doubt that Storey had planned to take the life of Sarah Howard that cold February evening, or that he had in fact taken a hammer to her head in an effort to cover up a guilty secret.

The testimony of tram driver Albert Woodley provided the crucial evidence that Sarah Howard had travelled to the area of the Bourne Bridge on Wherstead Road – not far from the murder scene – some fifteen minutes before 8.30 p.m. Woodley had known Howard as a conductress and stated that she had boarded his tram in the centre of town and took a seat on the left side of the vehicle, just inside the door. He had nodded to her and she had smiled back. He remembered her talking to his conductor Herbert Burgess just before she left the tram at 8.16 p.m.

Burgess backed up his colleague's account. He recounted seeing a woman he did not know boarding the car and riding as far as the Black Bridge on Wherstead Road, where she got off and walked in the direction of the Bourne Bridge. He recognised the woman as Sarah Howard from a photograph presented to him. He described her as being 'deep in thought.'

Albert Woodley's testimony also placed Storey in the same vicinity. He claimed to have seen his tram driver colleague outside the Lifeboat Inn on Wherstead Road at 8.18 p.m., walking in the direction of the Bourne Bridge. He further recalled seeing the accused a second time, at 9.10 p.m., as the tram made a return journey along Wherstead Road. He maintained that he had shouted across to him, saying, 'Hallo Fred. Did you have a good time?' in reference to the rumours he had heard about Storey carrying on with the housekeeper. His colleague had apparently ignored him.

In defending Storey, Mr Leighton would claim later in the trial that it was Woodley's evidence alone that placed the accused on the Wherstead Road at 8.18 p.m. He argued simply that the witness had been mistaken. When Storey himself was called as a witness and cross-examined, he said that he had been in the Cornhill area of the town at that time. From a jury's perspective, it was his word against Woodley's.

What did not seem to be in dispute was the fact that Storey had been walking from the direction of the Bourne Bridge later in the evening around the time that Woodley had stated. When called to give his evidence, PC Snell said that he had met Storey near Purfleet Street shortly after 9.15 p.m., coming from that direction. The accused had his hands in his pockets and Snell said that they had talked for a short while, before walking in the direction of Storey's home in Gower Street. Altogether, he had spent some ten minutes in his company passing the time of day before bidding him goodnight.

This was of course consistent with the statement that Storey had given earlier to DI Wood and tied in with the time that Myra Storey and her friend Ivy Woollard claimed that he had arrived home. And from the point of view of the prosecution this was to be expected – it was Mr Gill's view that the murder had already been committed by this time and Storey was heading home to clean himself up. Accepting this hypothesis, we are back to the question of the tram driver's composure. It must have taken some confidence to chat amiably to a patrolling police officer for ten minutes having just bludgeoned a woman to death and carrying the bloodstained murder

Ipswich.
Wherstead Rd.
Tram Terminus

Wherstead Road, Ipswich, along which Sarah Howard travelled by tram on the night of the murder.

weapon. PC Snell knew Storey and testified that he appeared that night to be 'sullen' and 'deep in thought.' That said, we can only conjecture that the motorman's demeanour had not given him any particular cause for alarm.

The evidence given to demonstrate Storey's alleged affair was, at best, inconclusive. Tram driver Bernard Griss claimed to have heard the rumours and said that he had seen Fred Storey waiting in the area of Howard's Beaconsfield Road lodgings on several occasions. During one encounter, he had apparently asked Storey if he had been 'after it again,' to which his colleague had put up his finger as if to say, 'keep it dark.' Cross-examined, Griss could not name a single week or month when any of this had occurred and could only say that it had been 'during the last year.' His account of the exchange with Storey also differed from the testimony he had given during the earlier coroner's inquest.

Violet Quinton, a waitress at a local hotel, testified that she had seen Storey and Howard together outside the tram depot one night after 10 p.m. She had been a conductress at the time and had worked with Storey. She believed that Howard had been off-duty and waiting for the tram driver to finish. She said she watched the pair walk off together along Constantine Road towards the towing path of the River Orwell.

This was hardly concrete proof of any sexual relationship and had occurred over a year before. In any case, on the second day of the trial, the

The Bourne Bridge on Wherstead Road. Witnesses claimed to have seen Sarah Howard walking towards the bridge shortly after 8.15 p.m. on the night of the murder.

defence called tram driver Bert Hall into the witness box. He maintained that he had been with Violet Quinton at the time and flatly contradicted her account. When questioned, he said that he had never seen Storey with the deceased and had often observed his colleague walking along Wherstead Road during the evening. While this may have been a case of one mate sticking up for another, it called into question the validity of Quinton's observations.

Other testimony was equally unconvincing. Ellen Tubby of Beaconsfield Road said she had seen the two tram workers together one evening during July 1919, in the yard of the Halberd Inn. Frank Patrick, a tram conductor, claimed to have seen Howard talking to Storey for three or four minutes on the platform of his tram on 1 February 1920. Edith Adams, also of Beaconsfield Road, declared that she knew Howard by sight and had heard the rumours of her relationship with the tram driver. She told the court how she had boarded Storey's tram one Sunday evening and had challenged him about carrying on with a single woman. He had apparently become very angry and had snapped back with, 'Who told you that?' before slamming the door in her face. Henrietta Long, a widow who knew both Storey and Howard, testified to seeing the two talking on Storey's tramcar a few weeks before the murder. She said that she had spoken to Howard after this and the housekeeper had admitted that while she and Storey were 'very friendly,' there was nothing going on between them.

This was hardly the sort of evidence on which to convict a man and send him to the gallows; but worse was to come.

The court heard from a Mrs Lily Rose Woodley, who had lodged with Sarah Howard at No.33 Beaconsfield Road. She testified that in May 1919 a picture postcard had been delivered to Howard at the address. She had taken it upon herself to read the card and told the court that it had been signed 'F.S.' She then revealed that a fortnight later a letter had arrived, again addressed to Howard. Stumbling across the ripped remains of this shortly afterwards, she had, with apparent alacrity, reassembled the letter with a close neighbour and read it. Her recollection was that the note had read:

> My own dearest darling, just a few lines to let you know that I am leaving off early tonight (Friday). Meet me at the Royal William at half-past seven.
> I remain, yours very loving, Fred Storey (I am like a fish out of water).

As to what had happened to this letter, Woodley asserted that the pair had been startled by a knock on the door and had thrown the correspondence onto the fire.

It was surprising that Justice Darling had allowed this testimony in a murder trial. Without the correspondence it was little more than tittle-tattle. Mr Leighton objected, submitting that there was no evidence to prove that this letter had existed or that it had been destroyed. Mr Gill replied simply that he would not press the matter.

In his defence, Fred Storey maintained steadfastly that he had never been on terms of intimacy with Sarah Howard, had never written to her and had never waited around in the area of Beaconsfield Road. Mr Leighton argued that having heard all of the testimony on the matter, there was no evidence to support the theory that Storey had been 'carrying on' with the deceased.

The prosecution placed great emphasis on the medical and forensic evidence that the police had assembled, but even here there were inconsistencies and unresolved questions. Dr Hoyland, the Police Surgeon, provided detailed testimony on the nature of his medical findings. He said that when he first saw the body at 10.25 a.m., he had formed the opinion that death had occurred at least ten or twelve hours before. But when cross-examined by Mr Leighton he appeared to shift ground, saying that Sarah Howard might have been killed at about 5 a.m. that morning, having regard to the appearance of the body.

The Halberd Inn, one of a number of locations where witnesses claimed to have seen Fred Storey and Sarah Howard socialising together.

Dr Spilsbury had no such doubts in expressing his view that the frost found on the body clearly indicated that the victim must had been dead ten hours or more – but then he had not attended the scene.

Having completed his scientific analysis, Spilsbury gave evidence of finding red spots and smears at seventeen different places on Storey's mackintosh. His tests had showed these to be consistent with mammalian blood. There were also similar stains on a cardigan and the hammer, the shaft of which had the appearance of having been recently washed. Interestingly, when cross-examined, the forensic pathologist said that while there was no doubt that the blood on the newspaper recovered from Gower Street was human, he could not speak definitely about the blood on the mackintosh – there were also no bloodstains in the pockets of the coat and no traces of blood on the boots or the detachable shirt-front the detectives had recovered. In addition, he had found no stains on the sharp part of the hammer.

This was hardly conclusive proof and the defence did its best to counter any suggestion that the bloodstains were evidence of murder. In her testimony, Myra Storey said that her father had cut himself shaving on the Friday afternoon. He had been in his shirt sleeves and she had given him a plaster. This was consistent with what Storey had told DI Wood during his interrogation at the police station when first arrested and cautioned. Myra also contended that when her father had arrived back at the house around 9.20 p.m. on the night of the murder he had not acted strangely in any way and she had seen no bloodstains on him. She had also been present the next day when the investigators had searched the house. While she had watched them take away the various items for forensic examination, she had only seen blood on the newspaper and not on any of the clothes.

Mr Leighton continued in his attempt to undermine the reliability of the forensic evidence on the second day of the trial. He talked specifically about the bloodstains observed on the mackintosh, saying that they were merely spots and not what one might have expected from the garment of someone who had just battered a woman to death. He argued that Fred Storey had suffered from nosebleeds all of his life and it was more likely that the spots were the result of one of these.

It is reasonable to construe that this line of defence was well rehearsed, for when Storey himself was called to give evidence he stated categorically that the blood on both the mackintosh and his cardigan was from a recent nosebleed. Backing this up, Bertram Wragg – another of Fred's tram worker colleagues – recounted how he had been with Storey at the Steamboat Tavern on the Monday before the prisoner's arrest. He had noticed blood running from Storey's nose and had asked him about it, believing that someone had hit him. Storey had apparently replied, 'No, my nose has been bleeding, is it bleeding now?'

To firmly fix the notion of a nosebleed in the minds of the jury, Leighton then called Fred Storey's brother, Robert, to the stand. He of course maintained that his younger brother had suffered from nosebleeds since he was a boy.

The alleged murder weapon was also the subject of much debate. In response to a question from the judge, Dr Hoyland reaffirmed his view that the hammer taken from Storey's home had caused all of the wounds he had seen on Sarah Howard's body. The defence made no effort to deny that the hammer was Storey's, although in giving her evidence, his daughter Myra said that she had never seen it before the day of the search. Her eighteen-year-old brother, Frederick, was more obliging when questioned. He said that the family had a coal hammer in the house and one at the allotment – the weapon produced in court looked like the one they kept in a shed on the allotment. Questioned further, he added that he had last seen the hammer at the allotment some two weeks before the murder.

As part of the defence, Mr Leighton called Frederick Goodchild to give evidence. He stated that he had sold some rabbits to Fred Storey on Saturday, 24 January and told the court that the accused always used a knife and hammer to cut up the meat. Storey had apparently taken the rabbits away wrapped in a piece of newspaper. In his own evidence, the tram driver confirmed that he used the hammer when cutting up rabbits at home. He also said that he had used it to build the shed on the allotment, but had removed the tool from the site when he found that the shed had been tampered with.

More significantly, in his outline of the defence, Leighton challenged the claim that Storey's hammer had been used to kill Sarah Howard. He said the head of the hammer was 1 ¾ inches across and submitted that it was impossible that such an instrument could have caused a round hole a 1 inch in diameter in the woman's head.

While it was not mentioned as part of the defence, it is surprising that no one thought to point out how odd it was that the hammer had been found in the fire grate of Storey's kitchen along with the bloostained newspaper. If we are again to believe that the accused had acted with 'great self-possession' in trying to cover his tracks, we might have expected him to have removed both items from the fireplace early on the Saturday morning. He would then have had ample opportunity to dispose of such incriminating evidence on his way into work.

Of course it is difficult, if not impossible, to envisage what a murderer might or might not reason or contemplate in the aftermath of such an appalling crime. The defence tried to paint a picture of Fred Storey as a loving father and devoted husband of 'unimpeachable character'; one who was content to play with his children before bedtime and support his wife with housework when she had occasionally been bedridden and suffering from neuritis for the better part of the period between December 1919 and February 1920.

There was also the question of his general demeanour to consider. The defence made a play of the fact that so many witnesses had reported seeing no real difference in Storey's manner and behaviour from the Friday night to the Saturday lunchtime, when he was arrested and questioned. Was this evidence of an innocent man or symptomatic of the actions of a cool, calculating killer who was able to contain any inner turmoil he may have felt by carrying on with the routine humdrum of his daily life?

In his closing speech, Mr Leighton reminded the jury that the key question to ask was whether the prosecution had proved beyond reasonable doubt that Storey committed the crime. There was no question of mercy in this case, simply the administration of justice. The jury could not act on suspicion or conjecture. Given the speed with which the jury delivered its verdict, it seems that the twelve had entertained few doubts about Storey's guilt.

It was Lord Erskine, one of the great advocates in English legal history, who said, 'An impartial trial is the first and dearest privilege of every Englishman.' Justice Darling seemed content to overlook his need for impartiality when he declared, after hearing from the Foreman of the jury, that the verdict was justified by the evidence. Before passing the death sentence he went on to say:

> It was most painful for everyone engaged in the case to find a man of the prisoner's character in the past standing in the position in which he stood. It was entirely through giving way to his passions, deceiving his wife, doing that injustice to his family, and ultimately, in order to extricate himself from his trouble, deciding to take the life of that miserable woman.

Storey, who throughout the trial had appeared calm and collected, appeared unmoved when he heard the sentence and left the dock quietly in the charge of his warders. He maintained this composure in the days that followed – the *East Anglian Daily Times* reporting later that he had, 'borne up well during the time which elapsed between his sentence at Bury and the time of his execution.' He persisted in his innocence until the very end.

There were some calls in the press in the week that followed for a stay of execution. One letter reproduced in The *Star* on 4 June 1920, asked:

> Sir - May I have a little space to ask if some movement cannot be made to secure a reprieve for the condemned man now awaiting execution? The evidence adduced appears to be but circumstantial...

In the event, no reprieve or commutation was forthcoming and the execution took place on Wednesday, 16 June, behind the closed doors of Ipswich Gaol. The executioner was John Ellis, infamous for conducting the executions of over 200 convicted criminals, including Dr Crippen in November 1910. It took less than twenty seconds from the time when Storey walked from his cell to the drop of the scaffold for the execution to be completed.

The weight of circumstantial evidence in this case would probably lead most of us to believe that Frederick William Storey had been guilty of murder. As to whether the evidence delivered in that two-day period proved the matter beyond reasonable doubt, we can, and should, be much less certain.

The County Court and Gaol on St Helen's Street in Ipswich, where Fred Storey was hanged behind closed doors on Wednesday, 16 June 1920. In former times, criminals were hanged in public between the two towers shown in the picture.

6

THE CORTON OUTRAGE

Corton, 1920

As a pretty seaside village just north of Lowestoft, Corton has been a popular tourist destination for well over 150 years. In its hey-day it was a fashionable watering-hole for middle-class Victorians who would pay sixpence to walk around its four miles of paths, three lakes and well-kept floral gardens, and take afternoon tea just a short distance from the golden sands of the pleasure beach. But the village was also the scene of a shocking murder in the late spring of 1920, which stunned the local population and the detectives assigned to the case.

The morning of Saturday, 29 May was warm and dry in Corton, although the gathering storm clouds threatened to bring some rain and wind later that day. Twelve-year-old Edward Freeman, who lived at No.12 Church Lane, was keen to take advantage of the favourable conditions and headed down to Corton Pond, one of his regular fishing haunts, with school-friend Gilbert Woods. The pond was little more than a large depression in the ground, some 6 yards from the main Lowestoft to Corton road along Gunton Hill, and screened from passing traffic by the trees and thick undergrowth which surrounded its sandy banks. Having walked around the pond casting their lines into the water for almost an hour, and seeing nothing out of the ordinary, the two boys set off for home at 11.10 a.m., intent on resuming their fishing later that afternoon.

When they returned to the pond after lunch, the two boys had been joined by another school-friend, Herbert Hurrell. As the youngsters fished, Freeman saw what he thought was a sack in the pond and, picking

Corton village at the time of the murder.

up a long stick, began to poke at it. The object broke the surface of the water and the young angler realised with horror that he was poking at a small human hand. Having alerted the others to what he had seen, he then ran off into the village to inform the local constable of his gruesome discovery. The time was 2.30 p.m.

PC Bickers, who was stationed at Corton, arrived at the pond around 3 p.m. By this time the storm clouds over the coast had delivered the anticipated downpour and Bickers was soaked when he reached the scene. He could see a body floating face-up on the surface of the water at the north end of the pond. With some difficulty he negotiated the steep banks of the pond and entered the water to retrieve the body. It lay in less than 2ft of murky water, some 18in from the bank. There was no doubt that the person was dead, but Bickers was shocked to discover that he held the body of a young girl dressed in a blue skirt, white blouse and brown coat, with heavy boots and black stockings on her legs. He carried the corpse to the large covered pavilion of the Corton Pleasure Gardens to await the arrival of his superiors.

A message was sent to Lowestoft police station informing the detectives based there that a body had been discovered, although it was some hours before an officer and police surgeon could attend the scene.

When he heard the news and was given a description of the corpse at around 7 p.m., Detective Sergeant White evidently believed that he already knew who the dead girl might be. With a fellow detective, he went at once to No.2 Farrow's Yard, Factory Street, the home of William Howes and his two daughters, thirteen-year-old Edith Elizabeth and eleven-year-old Lucy Valentine. Finding only the youngest daughter at home, with no knowledge of the whereabouts of either her sister or father, the police officer asked Lucy to pass on the message that William was to report to Lowestoft police station as soon as he returned. He gave no other hint as to the nature of their enquiries.

At 8.25 p.m., when he reached the Corton Pleasure Gardens along-side Dr Wilson Tyson the police surgeon, White's hunch proved to be accurate and he recognised immediately that the body was indeed that of Edith Howes. Dr Tyson conducted a short preliminary examination of the body in one of the outbuildings of the gardens. A cursory search around the pond revealed no immediate clues as to the manner of the girl's demise, although the surgeon was able to ascertain that her death was the result of drowning and she had been 'outraged', or raped, prior to this. He asked for the body to be taken to the mortuary in Lowestoft for a full post-mortem.

William Howes arrived home at about the same time as White and Tyson were examining the body in Corton. Responding immediately to the detective's request, Howes presented himself at the enquiry office of the police station and announced to PC Rumsey that his oldest daughter was missing, before providing a full description of the girl. He went on to explain that Edith had a history of leaving home and in the past had taken to stealing her stepmother's money and sleeping out on Battery Green. If we assume there to be some truth in this, it may help to explain why the family was already known to Sergeant White and why the detective seemed to have such a strong belief that the dead girl was likely to be Edith Howes.

Revealing nothing of the discovery at Corton, PC Rumsey asked Howes to take a seat and await the return of Sergeant White. It was over an hour later that the forty-year-old was seen by the detective, who explained that he had just returned from Corton Pond and revealed that Edith's dead body had been found in the water earlier that afternoon. Displaying little emotion, Howes' only response was 'Oh!'

White went on to explain that the doctor who had examined the body had also found that she had been 'interfered with.' Again, Howes reply was a simple 'Oh!' and he remained impassive at the news. Questioned further, Howes gave an unconvincing account of his whereabouts earlier that day and claimed that he had last seen Edith alive at 'about ten o'clock' that morning on the corner of Duke's Head Street, making her way to the beach. After further questioning, he was examined by Dr Tyson, although the surgeon could see no signs of bloodstains on his clothing and found no visible scratches or cuts on his wrists or hands. While his suspicions had been aroused, Detective White could do little but allow Howes to leave the station and return home.

On Sunday, 30 May, Dr Tyson conducted a thorough post-mortem. He found that Edith had been well nourished at the time of death. Despite the absence of a hat, her body was fully clothed and there were no immediate signs that her apparel had been torn or disarranged. Rigor mortis had set in and Tyson could see a fine froth around her lips and nostrils. The left-hand side of the face and ear were also slightly bloodstained and a closer examination revealed two faint abrasions over the left cheek and one under the jaw on the same side. Above the left temple was a visible contusion 1½ inches in diameter. There were no visible marks of constriction around the neck.

Internally, the windpipe and lungs of the body were found to contain a watery fluid, consistent with drowning. Taking account of this and the visible signs of violence on the face, Dr Tyson concluded that the young girl had received more than one blow to the side of the head, before being placed unconscious in the pond and left to drown. He also stuck by his original assertion that Edith had been raped prior to the drowning.

Baffled by the circumstances of the crime and unsure of Edith's movements in the hours leading to her death, the Lowestoft detectives began a full-scale murder investigation. Top of their suspect list was William Howes. Their enquiries revealed that, to the outside world, Edith had appeared to be a devoted and happy daughter, described later by the press as 'a girl of bright disposition.' However, it would soon become apparent that away from prying eyes Edith's home life had been anything but cheerful.

On the Monday morning the head teachers of all the local schools were asked to find out if any of their pupils had seen Edith between 9.20 a.m. and 2 p.m. on the Saturday. To the disappointment of the investigators, no information was forthcoming.

Later that afternoon, an inquest was opened at the Court House in Lowestoft, chaired by the East Suffolk coroner, Mr L.H. Vulliamy. Alongside the police and a small number of local people, William Howes was asked to appear. Given the unusual circumstances surrounding the case, Mr Vulliamy announced that he had summoned a jury to hear the evidence. He also sought to reassure the wider public, by declaring that deaths of this type were rare and that Lowestoft had a good record in terms of the small number of murders that had occurred in the town. As the police had not concluded their investigations, he proposed to take evidence only on the identification and discovery of the body.

The coroner's jury heard that the Howes family lived in a small rented cottage in the centre of town. Evidence was given by Emma Helen Tuttle, the fifteen-year-old daughter of William Tuttle, a next-door-neighbour to

Some of the key players in the drama: Detective Sergeant White (top left); Emma Helen Tuttle (bottom left); William John Howes (centre); PC Bickers (top right); and Lucy Valentine Howes (bottom right). (Lowestoft Heritage Workshop Centre)

A contemporary picture of Corton Road, Lowestoft, where Emma Tuttle claimed she had last seen Edith Howes alive.

the family. She explained that she had been sleeping at the Howes' cottage for the previous two months and having breakfast with the family each morning. Asked when she had last seen Edith alive, Tuttle deposed that after breakfast she had been delivering newspapers along Lyndhurst Road in Lowestoft and had paused briefly outside No. 22 at around 9.20 a.m. that Saturday morning. As she did so, she had seen Edith walking along Corton Road in the direction of the town. When asked, 'Was she with anyone?' Tuttle replied, 'She was with her father.' She was in no doubt about the identification.

The coroner said that no further questions were necessary at this point as plenty of time would be given to this at a later hearing. He then called PC Bickers to give evidence on the discovery of the body.

Bickers described his attendance at the crime scene. Asked if there were any visible signs of a struggle on the banks of the pond, Bickers admitted that as a result of the heavy storm that afternoon and the numerous foot-prints of the young anglers, he had been unable to detect any relevant marks in the soil. He was then asked a few more procedural questions before the inquest was adjourned until 21 June, to allow for the ongoing police investigation.

News of the murder was quick to circulate around the close-knit com-munities of the town and nearby villages. There was predictable shock at the initial discovery of the young girl's body, although it would be some days before the full extent and horror of the crime would become public knowledge, provoking widespread anger and revulsion. In this post-war period, many people were still coming to terms with the impact of four years of global conflict and within a few weeks of the murder a tablet would be unveiled in St Bartholomew's Church in Corton, to the memory of those who had fallen in the Great War. And while most families could cite their own personal losses and continuing tragedies, the murder of young Edith Howes seemed to tap into the collective consciousness and vulnerabilities of a community already beset with much grief.

Facing considerable pressure to act swiftly in resolving the case, the police arrested William Howes on Tuesday, 1 June, before a full contingent of local press photographers. At the police station he faced the charge that he had 'feloniously, wilfully, and of malice aforethought' killed and murdered his daughter. His only reply to the charge was, 'I am not guilty.'

Edith's funeral took place the following day, her body being laid to rest in Lowestoft Cemetery, attended by a large number of local resi-dents. After a short service in the cemetery chapel, conducted by the Revd Evan C. Morgan, a number of floral tributes were laid on the grave. These included a wreath from the youngster's fellow pupils at

Lyndhurst Road, Lowestoft – Emma Tuttle claimed she was standing on the pavement outside this property when she last saw Edith Howes.

St Margaret's School on Ipswich Road and a bunch of white carnations dropped onto the coffin by Edith's grief-stricken younger sister, Lucy.

Continuing with their investigations on the Wednesday, the police held a number of identity parades before an increasingly long list of locals who claimed to have seen Edith on the day of her death. William Howes was also charged formally with the murder before the County Magistrates. Described later by the press as 'a dark complexioned man of medium build,' the fisherman looked visibly nervous as he stood before the bench, his hands shaking violently as he clutched the handrail in front of him.

When asked to give evidence for the police, Superintendent W.A. Newson said that they had been suspicious of Howes following the results of the post-mortem examination and explained that the father had failed to give a satisfactory account of his movements on the day of the murder. Several witnesses claimed to have seen Howes on Corton Road at the time the accused said he had been on Duke's Head Street. Responding to the officer's request, the magistrates remanded Howes in custody until Wednesday, 9 June, to allow the police more time to conduct their enquiries. The prisoner was taken away and transported to Norwich Prison.

A full description of the murder and its investigation appeared in the *Lowestoft Journal* on Saturday, 5 June. At this point, the detectives were

St Margaret's School on Ipswich Road, where Edith Howes was a pupil. This photograph was taken in the 1970s before the school was demolished. (Lowestoft Heritage Workshop Centre)

beginning to build up a comprehensive picture of the man now held in custody. William John Howes was born in Lowestoft in 1880 and in the early part of his working life had been a baker's assistant before joining the army to fight in the Boer War. While serving in South Africa he suffered from typhoid and malaria – in later years complaining of frequent headaches, which he blamed on these earlier illnesses. Returning to civilian life, he became a trawler-man and married twice, both wives dying prior to the First World War and leaving him to bring up three children.

With his previous military experience, Howes joined the Suffolk Regiment as a private at the outbreak of war in August 1914 and was sent to the Western Front. He fought at the Battle of Loos and was badly injured at the Second Battle of Ypres, when he was blown up and sustained head injuries. In 1915 he was posted to Egypt and in the following year served at Salonika alongside a Canadian regiment. Later he spent time in a field hospital on the island of Malta, suffering from both malaria and shell shock. After four years of active service he was invalided out of the army and declared medically unfit for further military duties.

Working again as a fisherman, Howes married his third wife, Rose, in December 1918. By this time, only Edith and Lucy continued to live with him. It was clear that he was not an easy man to live with, his frequent

Norwich Prison in 1931, which was housed in the former Britannia Barracks of the Royal Norfolk Regiment on Mousehold Heath, and where William Howes was held until his trial. (George Plunkett)

headaches and malaria attacks making him prone to odd and erratic behaviour. Rose would testify later that he suffered from paranoia, believing that people were after him and accusing his wife of seeing other men and trying to poison him. On one occasion, while the family were at his sister's house in Bungay, Howes had apparently gone out into the lane convinced that someone was out to get him and, seized by an attack, had fallen down in the road frothing at the mouth.

Having consulted a doctor about her husband's behaviour, Rose persuaded Howes to move the family to Ramsgate, to stay with another of his sisters. But while there, Howes accused his sibling of trying to poison him and putting a spell on him which affected his eyes. Leaving Ramsgate, the family moved back to Lowestoft and into the cottage in Farrow's Yard. Within a short time Howes was again accusing Rose of seeing other men and on 7 May 1920 she left home to live in Battle, Sussex, no longer able to tolerate his behaviour.

When Howes next appeared before the magistrates on Wednesday, 9 June, the proceedings were even shorter than at the first sitting. Superintendent Newson said he had been in contact with the Director of Public Prosecutions and had been instructed to apply for a further remand of the prisoner. When asked if he had anything to say, Howes requested a postage stamp to enable him to write a letter to his family. He was remanded to appear again on Wednesday, 23 June.

Running parallel to the criminal investigation, the coroner's inquest resumed on Monday, 21 June, at Lowestoft police station. Howes was again brought from Norwich Prison. As before, he appeared restless and uncomfortable, his face displaying a nervous tick as he sat through the early part of the proceedings.

Once the evidence from the previous hearing had been read out, the coroner recalled Emma Tuttle to answer further questions about the day of the murder. Tuttle expanded on her earlier testimony. She recalled how she and her brother Walter had eaten breakfast with William Howes and his two daughters that Saturday morning. She and Lucy had then left after breakfast to deliver newspapers. At around 9.15 a.m., both girls had apparently seen Edith walking along North Parade towards Gunton Cliff. She had been wearing a knitted yellow tam-o'-shanter hat and had waved at them. Tuttle had also seen William a short while later, following closely behind Edith. As she had testified in the first hearing, Tuttle then repeated that she had last seen Edith at around 9.20 a.m. walking along Corton Road with her father and heading into Lowestoft.

In answer to the further questions posed by the coroner, Tuttle revealed that she and Lucy had returned to Farrow's Yard at approximately 11 a.m.

She had not seen William Howes again until the evening, when he appeared at the top of Farrow's Yard at around 8 p.m. She heard him say to Lucy, 'Is Edith home yet?' to which Lucy replied, 'No.' She claimed that Howes then went off again. In her continuing testimony, Tuttle also said that she had seen no cuts or bruises on Howe's face at breakfast the next morning and revealed that Rose Howes, the stepmother, had been away for 'some weeks.'

The coroner then invited William Howes to question Emma. He asked her if she had seen him at the top end of Farrow's Yard at around 12.05 p.m. that Saturday, to which the teenager replied 'No,' before explaining that at the time she had been at Bushell's Stores at the end of Factory Street, getting her mother's grocery.

Schoolboy Edward Freeman was then questioned by the coroner about the discovery of the body in Corton Pond. He outlined the sequence of events leading to the sighting of the hand sticking out of the water and the calling of PC Bickers.

Florence Picon, of No.5 Farrow's Yard, was called next and explained how she had seen the father and daughter at the top of Rant's Score – only a short distance from Lyndhurst Road where Emma Tuttle claimed to have seen the pair – at approximately 9.20 a.m. William had been talking to a man she did not recognise. Some ten minutes later, when she had returned home, she saw William and Edith again, back in Farrow's Yard. She described how they were talking closely and went silent as she approached, both ignoring her call of 'good morning.' It was her view that Howes had been scolding his daughter and she described Edith as looking pale and serious. However, when asked about the relationship between the two, Mrs Picon said she did not believe that the girl was afraid of her father and was nearly always to be seen with him. She believed Edith was very much attached to William.

A succession of witnesses then testified about seeing one or both of the pair throughout the course of the Saturday morning. Twelve-year-old Arthur Bindred, of Factory Street, said he had seen Edith standing outside

Corton Long Lane at the time of the murder. A number of witnesses claimed to have seen both Edith and William Howes walking along this route on the day of the murder. (Lowestoft Heritage Workshop Centre)

Blower's fish shop at around 10 a.m. The man with her was holding her wrist with one hand and had the other on her back. Edith was crying and it looked as if the man was trying to persuade her to do something or go somewhere against her will. Arthur had recognised Edith, but could only describe the man as being of 'middle size.'

James Freeman, a labourer for the Lowestoft Corporation, maintained that he had seen the pair on Corton Road at around 10.45 a.m. or 11 a.m. as he was walking from Corton to Lowestoft. He saw them approaching when he got to Gunton Hill and described how the young girl was walking with a limp some 5 or 6 yards behind the man. She was wearing a yellow tam-o'-shanter. Having greeted the man with 'good morning; it's rather warm,' Freeman had received the simple reply, 'Yes.' Questioned further, Freeman described the girl's coat as 'a dark one' and the man he had seen as 'a short man' who was wearing a cap and looked like a fisherman. However, he admitted that he could not swear the man he had seen was Howes.

Clemence Giles testified that she had been walking up Corton Long Lane with two other ladies at around 11 a.m. They had met a man walking down the lane near the railway bridge, closely followed by a young girl. The latter seemed tired and was walking with a limp. Giles described the girl as wearing a thick brown coat, heavy boots and black stockings and some form of hat (she was unable to remember what sort). The child was also carrying a small parcel, and there was some speculation later in the proceedings that this was the wrapped bread and butter sandwich that William had prepared for Edith's lunch. Giles explained that she was quite sure the man she had seen that day was William Howes – she had picked him out of the identity parade on Wednesday, 2 June.

Gwendoline Ellis, one of Giles' companions that day, was also able to confirm what the girl had been wearing and stated that the hat was a tam-o'-shanter. She too said that the girl had walked as if she were tired. Ellis described the man they had seen as wearing a dark cap and dark coat. However, unlike her companion, she was not sure that it had been Howes and had failed to pick him out during the same identity parade.

The vigilance of the local population appeared to be strengthening the case against Howes. John Robert Mann, a rag and bone collector, described seeing a man and girl on Corton Road when he was driving his donkey and cart. This was around 11.10 a.m. He confirmed that the body he had been shown at the mortuary was the girl he had seen that day. He described her as 'limping along' towards Corton with a man following some 100 yards behind her. She had been wearing a hat and when questioned further, Mann added, 'Yes, one of those woollen hats.'

Bertha Day, a manageress at the refreshment rooms in Corton Gardens, had also spotted the pair and had picked Howes out of an identity parade. She described the young girl as looking very distressed and tired, as if in pain. She too recalled seeing a hat, although she believed this to be black in colour.

Evidence for the possible time of the attack on Edith Howes came from a number of local youngsters who had been playing on the Common close to Corton Road. Fourteen-year-old John Rose from Lowestoft said that between 11.30 a.m. and 11.45 a.m. he had seen a man walking across the Common from the direction of Corton. Rose had subsequently identified the man as William Howes. He said that he had seen two big scratches on the right-hand side of the man's face and a little blood on his lip. The man had also mopped his face as he was sweating heavily. Asked about the man's clothing, Rose described him as wearing a dark suit and said that one of his legs was wet up to the thigh. Shortly afterwards the teenager had lost sight of the man, although he saw him a few minutes later while searching for one of his friends. At that stage, the man was lying down in the hollow of a bush, breathing heavily, the scratches on his face again visible.

John Rose's testimony was corroborated by another lad, Harry Youngman, although the latter believed the scratches had been on the left, rather than the right-hand side, of the man's face.

Nine-year-old Dudley Rushmere of Holly Cottage, Corton, also recollected seeing a man pass close by him in the same area sometime between 11 a.m. and 12 p.m. on the Saturday. As he passed him, he saw that the man's face was bleeding. Rushmere described the man as short and fat and wearing a dark jacket, cap and black boots.

The case against Howes was getting clearer and stronger. Having been invited by the coroner to give evidence, Edith's younger sister Lucy then took the stand. The sunburnt and chubby-faced child began by corroborating the statement given earlier by Emma Tuttle, adding that just after she had seen Edith for the last time, she had passed her father on the street. When she asked him who he was looking for, William had apparently replied 'Edie' before walking off in the direction taken by her sister.

Lucy explained that she had returned home just before 11 a.m. Her father had appeared about an hour later. He had visible scratches on his face, although she had seen no blood. He also appeared 'hot' and disappeared upstairs in the cottage. When he came down sometime later, Lucy had asked where Edith was. Her father said she had gone down to the sea and after preparing some lunch for them both, asked Lucy to go and look for her sister on the South Beach.

Lucy's fruitless mission to find her sister ended in the late afternoon and she returned home at around 5 p.m. to find the cottage empty. Her father arrived back a short time after this saying that he had been to the cinema. Lucy then testified that while the pair were having their tea, her father had walked up and down the room persistently, stopping every so often to glance at his face in a looking glass. After their meal, Howes had again left the cottage to go out, leaving her alone at the time when Detective Sergeant White called.

As he had throughout the proceedings, the coroner then invited William Howes to question the witness. Howes asked his daughter some questions about the police visit and appeared visibly more emotional than he had been during the earlier part of the inquest.

The next witness to be called helped to shed further light on Howes' emotional state and some of the events that had occurred prior to the murder. Eustace Leigh Trafford, an Assistant Secretary to the Lowestoft War Pensions Committee, said that he knew the accused and had met Howes at around 9.30 a.m. on the Saturday morning on the corner of Duke's Head Street. This was the man that Florence Picon had seen with Howes at that time. Trafford recalled seeing a young girl with Howes. When he asked the former soldier how he was, Howes had replied, 'Rotten' before explaining that he had heard from his wife that she was not coming back.

Trafford told the inquest jury that in his professional capacity he had met Howes a number of times since 1918 and retained a number of the man's personal documents. The ex-serviceman had been discharged from the army as a result of his neurasthenia, or chronic mental and physical exhaustion. Before that weekend, Trafford had last seen Howes on 17 May, when the fisherman had asked him to take charge of his children so that he could go to sea. The Assistant Secretary had explained that he would need to refer such a request to a special branch of the 'Ministry' in London before he could assist him.

The remainder of the day was taken up with the evidence provided by the police. PC Rumsey outlined how Howes had presented himself at the enquiry office of Lowestoft police station on the Saturday evening before his interview with Sergeant White. He then testified how he had accompanied White on a search of No.2 Farrow's Yard on Tuesday, 1 June. While there the officers had found a pair of dark trousers hanging up in an upstairs room of the cottage. These were produced for the jury. When discovered, the bottom of the trousers had been damp to the touch as far as the knee. There was also some fine white sand clinging to them.

Detective Macrow had been present during the post-mortem examination. He presented the jury with the clothes that had been found on the dead body of Edith Howes – a brown coat and frock, a pair of blood-stained bloomers, undergarments, stockings and a pair of black boots. Interestingly, no explanation was given for the missing hat which so many of the witnesses remembered Edith wearing on the day of her murder. The detective explained that fine white sand had been found on most of the items before them. Macrow had also helped White and Rumsey to search the fisherman's cottage and described finding a blood-stained rag in a coal cupboard which showed signs of stiffening. A further bloody rag was found on the stairs and a third on the windowsill of the living room.

Detective Sergeant White gave evidence about being notified of the death on the Saturday, visiting Farrow's Yard, attending the crime scene and interviewing Howes later that night. He outlined the convoluted account given by Howes of his whereabouts on the day in question. This ended with the father claiming to have been in the area of Battery Green and the fish market for most of the morning until about 11.30 a.m. and returning home around 12.05 p.m. Somewhat bizarrely, Howes had mentioned that he had been planning to take Edith to the doctor for putting 'celluloid stuff' in his cigarettes.

White gave further details of the interview with Howes that Saturday night. Asked at one stage if he realised Edith was dead, Howes had apparently responded by saying, 'That wench has brought some trouble on my shoulders.' When questioned further about his activities on the Saturday morning, Howes could not name anybody he had spoken to or anyone who might have seen him. Similarly, he could recollect no shops or other premises he had been into. Perhaps unsurprisingly, his recollection of events after lunch was much better and he claimed to have had a drink in the Volunteer Stores and Greyhound public houses with his father-in-law, Mr Farman. He also told of conversations with at least three people before he went to the cinema and ventured home at about 5 p.m.

When searched that night, White pointed out that Howes had clearly been wearing different clothes to those he had had on earlier in the day. In his pockets the detectives had found six letters written to him by his wife, Rose, from an address in Battle, Sussex – the most recent bearing the date of 18 May.

With the questioning of the police concluded, the coroner announced that he had been in contact with Dr Bernard Spilsbury of St Bartholomew's Hospital in London. On 12 June, Superintendent Newson had personally delivered a number of pieces of evidence to the eminent pathologist for

SIR BERNARD SPILSBURY.

When arsenic has closed your eyes,
  This certain hope your corpse may rest in:—.
Sir B. will kindly analyse
  The contents of your large intestine.

MR. PUNCH'S PERSONALITIES.—LXIV.

A 1928 engraving of Dr Bernard Henry Spilsbury of St Bartholomew's Hospital in London. The honorary forensic pathologist to the Home Office gave evidence at the Coroner's Inquest into the death of Edith Howes. (Wellcome Library, London) detailed forensic examination. This included the blood stained rags and a tablecloth found at No.2 Farrow's Yard. The coroner explained that due to the doctor's heavy workload, it had not been possible for him to attend the day's hearing. As a result, the inquest would be adjourned until Thursday, 8 July, in order to allow Dr Spilsbury to present his findings.

While the proceedings of the inquest had proved to be both enlightening and lively, events outside had been no less dramatic – from 5 p.m. onwards huge crowds had lined the main approaches to the police station, each spectator hoping to get a glimpse of the reviled child-killer. When Howes was finally led away at around 7 p.m. that evening, he had to be bustled into a waiting cab and driven quickly to the railway station for his journey back to Norwich.

On Wednesday, 23 June, Howes appeared before a further session of the local magistrates. Outside he was greeted once more by an angry mob. The accused stepped smartly before the bench and sat down immediately, before being asked by the presiding magistrate, Mr L.J. Peto, to stand back up again. He jumped up and clutched the handrail nervously, his face twitching as it had done during the coroner's inquest. Having travelled over 30 miles from Norwich to attend the session, Howes was told only a few minutes later that he was remanded to appear again before the magistrates a week later.

By this stage, the murder story had been taken up with some relish by a cadre of local and national journalists, each twist and turn of the investigation filling sizeable columns of the *Lowestoft Journal* in particular. In the same week as the account of Howes' appearance before the coroner's jury was reported, another seaside tale was the talk of the town – this one providing some much-needed relief from the disturbing revelations of the Corton Pond tragedy. Following the prompt and fearless action of eleven-year-old Hilda Keller, a young lad of five who was unable to swim had been saved from drowning in the sea off Lowestoft. It was reported that Keller had been changing to go home after bathing when she heard the cries of William Thomas Wilkinson on the North Beach. Responding immediately, she plunged into the sea fully dressed and rescued the drowning boy from certain death. The youngster was widely applauded for her selfless act of bravery.

On Wednesday, 30 June, the judicial process ground on relentlessly with a further remand hearing before the magistrates at the Lowestoft Police Court. Howes was unshaven and displayed all his usual symptoms of nervousness, although he appeared to be more attentive in following the evidence being presented. Harold Pearce, representing the Director of Public Prosecutions, opened the hearing and outlined the main facts of the case.

Henry Charles William Blyth, an architect and surveyor, was called to provide the magistrates with a plan of the various locations involved in the case. He explained that the distance from Duke's Head Street (where the accused claimed he had last seen Edith) to Corton Pond, via the railway bridge in Corton Long Lane, was 2½ miles. The distance from the fish market (where Howes said he had been at the time of the murder) was 2¾ miles. The implication was clear – if the various witness testimonies were accurate, Howes could not have been at either location at the times he claimed.

The magistrates were then shown some photographs of the crime scene taken by Lowestoft photographer George William Anger, who worked for Boughton & Son. One showed the dead body of Edith Howes. The remaining evidence came from the same assembled cast that had already testified at earlier sessions of the coroner's inquest. With the police, officials, witnesses, advocates and journalists struggling to keep up with who had said what at which hearing, we can be certain that William Howes was completely lost given his highly visible and fragile mental state.

Only PC Rumsey and John Mann, the rag and bone merchant, added new information to their earlier statements. Rumsey was asked if he had noticed Howes' boots at the time the accused arrived at the enquiry office of the police station. The officer responded positively: 'They had the appearance of having been recently cleaned.' Mann asserted that he had seen Howes a second time on the day of the murder and described how he and his wife had watched the fisherman pass by their house in Chapel Street at around 5 p.m. Mann had asked his wife, 'Do you know that man going there?' to which she had replied, 'Yes, he lives on Factory Street.' Mann had apparently responded by saying, 'If I didn't see him on the Common with that little girl it beats me.'

The court hearing ended with yet another adjournment, a further sitting being planned for Friday, 9 July. In the event, the additional session was not required as the coroner's inquest concluded on the day before this, its jury returning a verdict of 'wilful murder' against Howes and committing him to appear for trial at the next assizes to be held in the county. In recognition of the lengthy and convoluted nature of the enquiry they had endured, the jurors were given exemption from any further jury service for three years.

The final session of the coroner's inquest had added only a few basic facts to what already appeared to be a watertight case against the accused. Nevertheless, the proceedings attracted widespread publicity as a result of the attendance of a star witness – the honorary forensic pathologist to the Home Office, Dr Bernard Spilsbury.

In presenting his evidence at the inquest, Dr Spilsbury was succinct but damning in the case against William Howes. He explained that he had received a number of items for testing on Saturday, 12 June. His microscopic examination of the clothes, rags and tablecloth retrieved from No.2 Farrow's Yard had revealed clear traces of human blood. The pathologist had concluded that these stains were no more than two weeks old – the timing fitting in exactly with the date the crime had occurred.

The trial at the Suffolk Assizes was held on Wednesday, 28 October 1920. Recognising the overwhelming strength of the case against their client and the certainty of a death penalty if he was found guilty, the defence team sought to demonstrate that Howes was of 'an unsound mind' at the time when the crime had been committed.

William's wife, Rose Howes, was called to give evidence for the first time. She explained that her husband suffered from attacks brought on by malaria and would often say things to her that he would not remember later. These attacks could sometimes last for two weeks, although during that time he had never been known to hurt the children. Challenged by the prosecution, Rose admitted that Howes had hit her and had once thrown her belongings out into the yard. She also said that she had once gone to Lowestoft police station to complain about her husband's physical abuse, although the officers had taken no action. Pressed about whether she had ever said to the police that Howes was 'out of his mind,' Rose could only answer, 'No.'

The defence next called Howes' sister, Julia Freestone, in an attempt to establish that there was a history of mental illness in the family. Freestone told the court that their mother had died in an asylum. She also described her brother's erratic behaviour when the family had lodged with her in Bungay from February to Easter 1918. This included his frequent claims that his wife was putting poison in his food and cigarettes.

Dr J.R. Whitwell of St Audry's Hospital in Melton, gave evidence in support of Freestone's testimony. He explained that Howes' mother had been an inmate of the asylum and had died there in 1913. He went on to say that he had also examined Howes and had concluded that he was suffering from 'delusional insanity' – his particular delusion being that his wife was acting unfaithfully and trying to poison him.

There was further medical testimony to support the view that Howes was suffering from a mental illness. Dr W. Fryer, the Medical Officer for Norwich Prison, stated that he had examined the prisoner during his detention and had made a report to the Home Office concluding that Howes would not have been responsible for his actions at the time of committing any such crime. Similarly, Dr Dudley William Boswell from

Lowestoft testified that the prisoner had been placed under his care in early 1920 suffering from delusions. On one occasion Howes had apparently believed that he could see a beetle in his wife's throat. The doctor had no hesitation in asserting that Howes had an unsound mind.

Having heard all of the evidence, the jury took an hour to return a verdict of 'Guilty' against Howes, the statement read out by the foreman expressing hopes that the prisoner would be shown some mercy on the grounds of his physical and mental condition. With little option but to respond in the prescribed manner, the trial judge then passed the sentence of death on the trawler-man, agreeing to pass on the recommendation for mercy to the appropriate authorities. Howes was then removed from the dock and transported to Ipswich Prison to await his execution.

This sad and sorry case had one final twist to keep the story firmly in the public gaze. In November 1920 it was reported that the recommendation for mercy forwarded to the Home Secretary had been successful and Howes' death sentence was to be commuted to one of detention at his Majesty's pleasure. In reply to a letter recommending mercy from the Lowestoft branch of the Missions to Seamen, the Home Office responded by saying:

Ipswich Prison, where William Howes was held after his conviction awaiting execution.

DAY-ROOM FOR MALE PATIENTS.

An engraving of the day-room for male patients in the Broadmoor Criminal Lunatic Asylum, where William Howes was kept until his death in 1943. (Wellcome Library, London)

Sir, - with further reference to your letter on behalf of William John Howes, now in the prison at Ipswich under sentence of death, I am directed by the Secretary of State to inform you that after medical enquiry into the mental condition of the prisoner, he has advised his Majesty to respite the capital sentence with a view to the immediate removal of the prisoner to the Broadmoor Criminal Lunatic Asylum.

William Howes was transferred to Broadmoor later that month. He was to spend the rest of his life institutionalised and died on Wednesday, 18 August 1943.

7

THE ARBOR LANE TRAGEDY

Pakefield, 1925

In the early part of December 1925, the east coast of England was gripped by some thick and persistent downfalls of snow and ice which were to take several days to thaw and clear. And when the dead body of twenty-one-year-old Lilian Evelyn France was discovered lying in the snow in Arbor Lane, Pakefield, in the early morning of Thursday, 10 December, it was difficult to know whether she had expired as a result of the inclement weather or had in fact lost her life as a result of something more sinister. The initial medical examination at the scene provided no greater clarity, with local surgeon Dr Harold Barraclough reserving judgement on the likely cause of death until a post-mortem examination had been carried out. It was only later in the day that the authorities realised that what they were dealing with was indeed a heartrending case of foul play.

The body was discovered at around 6.30 a.m. that morning by milkman Henry David Burlingham while on his delivery round. He found the young woman lying face-up and fully-clothed in a partly-opened gateway by the roadside. Naturally alarmed, Burlingham made for the nearest property, that of Ernest Arthur Smith, a Pakefield schoolmaster. There he saw the maid, Beryl Vale, who communicated the news to her employer. Ernest Smith asked Vale to go to the house of Arthur Wightman, the local police constable, to get his assistance. Having done this, he ventured outside to view the body, which lay only 35ft or so from his bungalow on the south side of the lane. He could see that the dead woman's head was pointed towards the gate, with her legs facing the direction of his garden.

Her right arm was fully extended, the other partly so, and both hands were open and gloved. He touched the body momentarily to make certain that the young woman was dead.

Arbor Lane was part of a circular walk popular with summer visitors to the seaside resort and used all year round by locals. Most walkers would travel out from the centre of Lowestoft by tramcar to dismount at the Pakefield terminus which was situated along London Road (now close to the site of the Tramway Hotel). They would then follow Pakefield Street or Florence Road to the cliffs nearby, returning to the tram station via Arbor Lane. As a result of some property development in the post-war period, a few bungalows had sprung up in the area – the original thoroughfare being little more than a farm track. Despite this, it still retained the feel of a quiet country lane. Perhaps it was no surprise that the route was also popular with youngsters and courting couples.

PC Wightman joined Ernest Smith at the scene some twenty minutes after the body had first been found. He observed a thin red mark on the neck of the deceased almost 4in in length. He also saw a small piece of brown cloth clinging to the barbed wire which ran along the top of the gate. It matched that of the coat the woman was wearing. There were also heel marks in the mud close to the gate which looked to have been made by the shoes on her feet. Most significantly, he saw that beside the body were a hat and a handbag. Examining the contents of the bag, he found a receipt for £1 12s 5½d made out to a 'Miss France, "Eversfield", Kirkley Cliff Road.'

Wightman telephoned the main police station in Lowestoft and communicated the news of the death to Police Sergeant Pearsons, before putting in a call to Dr Barraclough. Having then remained with the body, he was joined by the pair just after 8.30 a.m. Both men were quick to spot the red mark on the neck of the deceased. Pearsons also noted that the woman's teeth were clenched and the tip of her tongue was protruding slightly. He could see that her shoes were covered in mud and the heels were almost torn off.

Dr Barraclough made his own observations, but did not, at this stage, share them with the officers present. However, in view of the suspicious red mark on the neck, he asked them to make arrangements for the body to be taken into Lowestoft for a post-mortem examination. As a temporary measure, they carried the corpse to the garage of Ernest Smith's bungalow, where it remained for a short while away from the public gaze.

It was now becoming clearer from events close-by, that the body was that of the young woman named on the receipt. Lilian Evelyn France lived at the address in Kirkley Cliff Road and was employed as a domestic serv-

Arbor Lane, Pakefield, where the dead body of Lilian Evelyn France was discovered on the morning of Thursday, 10 December 1925.

'Eversfield' on Kirkley Cliff Road, Pakefield, where Lily France worked as a domestic servant.

ant by a Mr and Mrs Sargeant. She had left her lodgings at about 7 p.m. the previous evening – Wednesdays being one of her two regular evenings off – saying that she would be back home by 9.30 p.m. that night. When her absence had been discovered early the next morning, a concerned Mrs Sargeant had telephoned the police and also sent a telegram to Henry France – the girl's father – little realising that the body of her employee had already been found a short distance away.

Following up on the name and address written on the receipt, PC Wightman arrived at Eversfield later that morning and had the unenviable task of informing the distressed Mrs Sargeant about the discovery of the corpse. But worse was to come. Henry France had cycled over from Kessingland to Kirkley Cliff Road on receiving the telegram about his missing daughter. On his journey he had already had one significant encounter which must have raised concerns in his mind about the well-being of his daughter. The details of this unexpected meeting with a young man called Harold George Waters, at around 10.20 a.m., would only emerge later. That said, he must still have been thunderstruck on arriving at Eversfield, meeting PC Wightman and being told the news of his daughter's demise. The police officer had accompanied Mr France back to Arbor Lane, where the distraught father confirmed that the body was that of his daughter.

From that moment on, the police began to build up a clear picture of the young woman that everyone had known as Lily. She was one of five daughters born to Mr and Mrs Henry France. Her father, originally from London, was a retired coastguard who had settled with the family in Kessingland following his period of service. The couple's youngest child had passed away through illness at the age of nine, only months before the tragedy of Lily's untimely death. The three surviving girls were Caroline, Ruby and Lily's twin-sister, May Beatrice.

Lily had worked for the Sargeants for over two years. She was regarded as a reliable and trustworthy employee and was viewed as quiet and pleasantly-spoken. She was described in one later newspaper account as 'a fine, well-built girl, who was generally liked.' Outside of work, she was closely associated with the Girls' Friendly Society, and was highly esteemed in both the Lowestoft and Kessingland branches of the movement. The society – which still exists today – was established in 1875 as part of the Anglican Church to promote chastity among working class girls and became a popular and pioneering youth movement, claiming around 200,000 members by the outbreak of the First World War.

For the previous nine months, Lily was known to have been keeping company with Harold Waters, an eighteen-year-old man who lived with

A membership certificate for the Girls' Friendly Society of which Lily France was an active member.

his parents on Beresford Road in Lowestoft and who worked as a part-time attendant at an ice rink in the town. The details of their romance would emerge later, but it soon became clear that it was Waters who Lily France had planned to meet up with on the evening of Wednesday, 9 December.

Following the discovery of the body, all available detectives and uniformed officers in the Lowestoft area had been deployed in an effort to find clues that could establish the cause of the young woman's death. It did not take long for a vital piece of the jigsaw to fall into place. Just after

11 a.m. on the Thursday morning, Harold Waters walked into Lowestoft police station and, being greeted by Sergeant Pearsons, announced, 'I think you want me?' When asked what for, he replied, 'For the murder of Lily France.'

Pearsons cautioned the youngster and took him through into an office that was being used to co-ordinate the enquiries into Lily's death. There they were joined by Detective Sergeant H. Clarke. The detective explained who he was and said to Waters, 'Lilian France has been found dead in Arbor Lane, Pakefield. I understand you have made a statement to Sergeant Pearsons.' He then repeated what Waters had said earlier, asking him if he wanted to add anything to this. Waters replied, 'I have no more to say. I'm guilty, and there you are.' On the basis of this apparent confession, Waters was charged with wilful murder later that evening and detained in the police cells overnight. On being searched, he was found to

A photograph of the old Lowestoft police station taken in the early 1970s. Harold George Waters entered the station on Thursday, 10 December 1925 and apparently confessed to the murder of Lily France. (Lowestoft Heritage Workshop Centre)

have on him some letters from Lily France and a green pocket handkerchief that she had owned.

Dr Barraclough conducted his post-mortem examination that afternoon in the presence of Dr Wilson Tyson, the police surgeon. His report was received by Sergeant Pearsons at around 7 p.m. that evening, just before the decision was taken to charge Waters with the murder. During his initial examination at the crime scene, he had found the face of the deceased swollen and the tip of her tongue pressed against the upper teeth and protruding slightly from the mouth. A thin line of blood had been visible below the right nostril and the red mark around Lily's neck was found to be about 6in in length. On turning the body over, the surgeon had found that the coat had been ripped across the back. He had also observed two distinct tracks in the mud, which he imagined had been caused by the heels of the dead woman's shoes, for they ended close to where her feet had been.

The post-mortem revealed a line – a quarter of an inch thick – running around the neck of the victim at the level of the upper part of the thyroid at the front, and extending slightly upwards at the back of the neck. The wound had filled with blood. The eyelids of the body were similarly puffed-up. There was a thin mark on the back of the right wrist and some swelling there also. On the upper part of the breastbone, the surgeon found some bruising. Internally, the heart was found to be considerably engorged, although Barraclough observed the valves and muscles to be generally sound. The lungs too were full of blood and there was some subpleural haemorrhaging within the body wall. His conclusion was that Lily France had died of asphyxia, due to strangulation.

The post-mortem had also revealed one other significant factor, given Lily's relationship with Waters and her membership of the Girls' Friendly Society. She had died a virgin, maintaining the chastity that was so clearly central to her faith.

There was much shock and dismay at the news of the murder in the Lowestoft area generally and the Kessingland community in particular, where the France family were well-known and much respected. For a couple of days, the case also attracted the attention of the national as well as the local press.

An inquest was opened at the Lowestoft Police Court before Mr L.H. Vulliamy, the East Suffolk coroner, at 4.45 p.m on the afternoon of Friday, 11 December. It was clear that news of the proceedings had become public knowledge, for a considerable crowd had gathered outside the building prior to the inquiry. When the door of the courtroom was opened there was such a scramble to get inside that the public seats were soon filled, and the police officers present had to lock the doors to prevent others from obtaining entry.

Having been sworn in, the jury of nine was first taken to view the body of the deceased in the mortuary. While they were absent, there was a tense silence in the courtroom broken only by the occasional, whispered conversation between the coroner and Police Superintendent W.A. Newson. When they returned, the jury was addressed by Mr Vulliamy, who briefly explained the nature of the case before them and how the inquest would proceed.

The coroner said that following his conversations with the police, he did not propose to hear any medical evidence at this stage, preferring instead to adjourn the inquest to the end of the month to enable the magisterial inquiry into the death to be completed, where there was every likelihood that a criminal charge would be brought against someone for the death. He added that this approach was in line with the spirit of the new Coroner's Bill, which contained the following provision in Section 17:

> If on an inquest touching a death the coroner is informed before the jury have given their verdict that some person has been charged before examining justices with murder, manslaughter or infanticide of the deceased, he shall in the absence of reason to the contrary, adjourn the inquest pending the conclusion of the criminal proceedings.

He did, however, wish to hear evidence on the finding of the corpse and its identification, so that the body could be released for burial. He then told the jury that he understood the deceased woman had been keeping company with a man called Harold Waters, who was being held in custody and was later to appear before the local magistrates. He further understood that on the advice of his solicitor – Mr Geoffrey Bracey – the accused would not be present at the inquest.

The jury then heard the short testimonies of Henry France and PC Wightman, with the coroner explaining that both would be called to provide further evidence at the resumed inquiry. He then adjourned the inquest until 31 December.

Immediately after the adjournment, Harold Waters was brought before Mr Lancelot Orde, a county magistrate. Waters was a tall youth, with a somewhat pale complexion and dark hair brushed back from his forehead. As he entered the courtroom he had the suspicion of a smile on his face, but this quickly disappeared as he began to take in what was going on around him. He cast a swift glance at the courtroom clock and then fixed his eyes on the magistrate for the remainder of the short hearing.

Sergeant Pearsons gave brief details of how he had gone to Arbor Lane to view the body and then described how Waters had arrived at the police station later that day and had given his statement about being wanted in connection with the murder of Lily France. He then described how the suspect had been charged with the murder at 7.30 p.m. that same evening. On this evidence, and at the request of Superintendent Newson, Lancelot Orde remanded the prisoner to appear before the magistrates on Thursday, 17 December. As the hearing was closed, Waters talked for a few seconds with Mr Bracey and then turned smartly to the right and left the court in the company of his warders. He would spend the next six nights locked up in Norwich Prison, housed in the former Britannia Barracks of the Royal Norfolk Regiment on Mousehold Heath.

The remains of Lily France were laid to rest in the peaceful village churchyard of Kessingland on the afternoon of the following Tuesday. Whether it was in deference to the wishes of her parents – that the ceremony should be a short and simple family affair – or due to the continuing wintry weather, there were only a handful of bystanders present at the burial. But throughout the length of the village there was every sign of the deepest sympathy felt by the community, with all curtains and blinds drawn long before the funeral cortege made its way from the France family home to the church of St Edmund.

Norwich Prison in 1931, where Harold Waters was held until his trial in January 1926. (George Plunkett)

The parish church of St Edmund in Kessingland, where Lilian Evelyn France was buried on Tuesday, 22 December 1925. (Tony Morley)

The service was conducted by the rector, the Revd H.P.F. Scott, and throughout the ceremony a thin, white, frosty mist hung over the burial ground like a shroud. The only family mourners were Lily's parents and her sisters Ruby and May. Among the floral tributes was one from a 'Mr and Mrs Waters and family' of Beresford Road, Lowestoft. History has not recorded how the France family reacted to this act of compassion from the parents of their daughter's killer.

Two days later Harold Waters appeared before the magistrates having been brought back by rail from Norwich. A large crowd awaited him outside the Lowestoft Police Court, but he was taken in by a side door to avoid any confrontation. At 11 a.m. he was called before the bench to face the charge against him. He appeared to have more colour than at the previous hearing and also seemed to follow the proceedings with greater interest. He was represented by Mr Gerald Dodson, instructed by Mr Bracey.

Mr G.C. Peevor, appearing for the Director of Public Prosecutions, provided an outline of the case and said that Waters had been keeping company with Lilian Evelyn France and was accused of killing the young woman by strangling her in Arbor Lane. The magistrates then heard testimony from some of the key witnesses.

Henry Burlingham described how he had found the body and reported his discovery to the maid of Mr Smith. Ernest Smith then testified about going out to view the corpse. In answer to a question from Mr Dodson, Smith confirmed that he had heard voices outside his home on the evening of 9 December, but asked if this included 'anything unusual at all' the schoolmaster had to concede, 'Nothing whatsoever.'

PC Wightman then gave his evidence, describing his attendance at the crime scene and what he had observed at the time. He said that the body had looked to be lying in a 'perfectly natural attitude' and confirmed that there were no signs that the clothing of the dead woman has been disarranged. In his view, her handbag had also not been opened or interfered with.

Dr Barraclough then provided an outline of the medical evidence, including his observations at the scene and the results of the post-mortem examination. He restated his view that the death was the result of asphyxia due to strangulation. He was challenged by Mr Dodson about this: 'Did you not, after the first examination, say at first that death was due to exposure and shock?' Barraclough snapped back, 'Never, in this world.' Dodson was not to be outdone, and next asked, 'Did you find anything upon or near the body which could account for the mark which you afterwards found as going right round [the neck]?' The surgeon could only reply, 'No.'

The final question put to Dr Barraclough concerned Lily France's chastity. Mr Dodson enquired, 'Was this unhappy girl a virgin?' to which Barraclough replied, 'Certainly.' His colleague at the post-mortem, Dr Tyson, then spoke to confirm being at the examination and said he concurred with the conclusions of his medical colleague.

The next witness called was Mrs Rosetta Foulger, a cook and housekeeper to Mr and Mrs Sargeant at Eversfield. She explained that she had been in their service since September 1923 and Lily France had worked at the house prior to her arrival. The housekeeper had seen Lily leaving the house at around 7 p.m. on the night of the murder and had been told that she would return no later than 9.30 p.m. The next morning, when she discovered that the maid had failed to return, Mrs Foulger had alerted Mrs Sargeant, who in turn had communicated with the police. Asked about Harold Waters, the witness said that she had seen him speaking to Lily on only one occasion.

When Lily's twin sister, May Beatrice, was called to testify, she explained that she had known Waters for about nine months. Mr Peevor was keen to explore the nature of the relationship between the prisoner and the deceased: 'Did you know he had been keeping company with your sister?' Miss France replied, 'I have seen him with her during the last three months.' When she was asked if she had seen her sister on the evening of the murder, May explained that they had met up a little before 7 p.m. on London Road South in Lowestoft, just opposite Ford's boot shop. Harold Waters had been with her and the three had talked for a while for the short time they were together. When May had left them they were heading towards Pakefield. It was the last time she had seen her sister.

Mr Dodson then asked, 'While you were with them, did they seem perfectly happy together?' May replied, 'Yes', and also answered in the affirmative to the question, 'Did your sister sometimes bring him [Waters] to your parent's house?' However, when asked if she knew that Lily had promised to marry Waters, May was emphatic in answering 'No' and confirmed that while Lily had mentioned an engagement she had said nothing about marriage.

Henry France was next to give evidence. He said that he had known the prisoner for a few months, as Waters had visited his daughter at their house in Kessingland. Asked to describe Lily, he said that she had been happy and bright, with 'a very nice disposition' and enjoyed 'very good health.'

The father was then asked to explain what had happened on the morning he received the telegram from Mrs Sargeant. He described how he had cycled from his home towards Lowestoft, reaching Pakefield School at about 10.20 a.m. As he did so, he spotted a young man walking along the road and saw that it was Harold Waters. He pulled over and dismounted to talk to him. Waters had seemed keen to walk on, but Mr France stopped him and told him about the telegram. When asked, the younger man had admitted being with Lily the previous evening, but when asked if he knew anything about her disappearance had given no reply. The pair had then walked together in silence as far as Wellington Road. At this point, Mr France had said, 'You have walked this distance and said nothing. Is it your intention to give me any information or not?' Waters had replied simply, 'No,' and the two men had parted at that point.

May France was then recalled to confirm whether some letters which had been found on Waters when he was searched at Lowestoft police station had been written by her sister. Having been shown the handwriting, she said that this was the case. The court was then read the contents of two of the letters. The first was dated 16 October 1925 and read:

My Dear Harold, - I certainly do wish we were married. I think you must have taken what I said the wrong way. I know we cannot be married, so it is just as well to leave it at that for the present, and if you look at it in the right light it is a great responsibility for anyone so young as we are. But still I hope the time will not be long...when we can have a little house of our own. It will seem like Heaven, darling. This is all I have time to write...Time Flies...

The second letter was dated 11 November:

Mr Darling Harold, - Many thanks for your letter received this morning... My dear, I do wish you could get a permanent job, then things would look more hopeful. As things are it does not seem we shall be in a position to get married at Christmas in twelve months. Well, we must hope for the best...

The remainder of the magistrates hearing was taken up with the testimony of the police officers, Sergeant Pearsons and Detective Sergeant Clarke. They were asked to give evidence on the alleged confession of the prisoner and his detention at Lowestoft police station. This concluded the case for the prosecution, and Mr Peevor then asked that the accused be committed to stand trial at the next assizes. When formally charged, Harold Waters said in a firm, clear voice, 'Not guilty, and I reserve my defence,' after which he was committed by the magistrates to face trial at the County Court.

When the inquest resumed on the afternoon of Thursday, 31 December, there was little fresh evidence to disclose other than a few additional medical details. In any event, there were few doubts about the likely outcome of the hearing. Harold Waters was present, having been brought up from Brixton Prison where he had been held over the Christmas period. His father sat in the public gallery.

The hearing again took evidence from Henry France and PC Wightman. Added to this were the depositions of Henry Burlingham, May France, Sergeant Pearsons, Detective Sergeant Clarke, Dr Barraclough and Dr Tyson.

In his summing up, the coroner said that he would not need to detain the jury at any length. He reminded them that their duty was not to prove the charge against the accused 'up to the hilt,' but to decide only whether this was a *prima-facie* case of murder that required the prisoner to be sent for trial. When the jury returned, having been absent from the courtroom for some twenty minutes, the foreman announced that they 'were unanimous in finding that the death was due to asphyxia from strangulation' and that their verdict was one of 'wilful murder' against Waters. However, they recommended that he be shown some mercy on account of his youth.

The accused had less than a month to wait until his trial. When he appeared before the Grand Jury at the Suffolk Assizes in Ipswich on Friday, 22 January 1926, Waters had just turned nineteen years of age. He was tried before Mr Justice Rowlatt (Sir Sidney Arthur Taylor Rowlatt), who had earlier chaired the controversial Rowlatt Committee, appointed by the British Indian Government in 1918 to evaluate the links between political terrorism in India, the German government and the Bolsheviks in Russia. This gave rise to the Rowlatt Act, an extension of the Defence of India Act 1915.

Mr J.F. Eastwood appeared for the Crown, with Mr Dodson once again acting for the defence. When asked how he pleaded to the charge against him, Waters replied, 'Not guilty.'

Unsurprisingly, the case for the prosecution covered much of the same ground as the early hearings. At its conclusion, Harold Waters was called to give evidence in his own defence. He explained that he had been engaged to Lily France and, prior to her death, the two had never had any serious quarrel. That night he had arranged to spend the evening with her, but, finding that he did not have enough money to take her to any place of entertainment, the two had gone for a walk. Entering Arbor Lane, they were still on affectionate terms and Waters had said that they should get married the following Christmas. He added that she had been quite agreeable to this suggestion.

Waters was then asked what had happened next. He paused for some time before answering, and then admitted, 'Well, we started quarrelling.' Mr Dodson asked what the argument had been about. Waters replied, 'She thought I was rather too young to get married.' The barrister then continued: 'And I suppose you thought you were not?' 'Yes,' said Waters, 'I lost my temper then. I was wearing a scarf at the time, and I put it round her neck and strangled her. Then she suddenly went limp and slid down to the ground.'

Mr Dodson then asked whether Waters had meant to do her any harm by placing the scarf around her neck. 'Yes,' said the accused. His defence counsel then put it to the jury that the act had been committed in the fury of the moment and was 'the outcome of a gust of temper.' It had happened 'in the twinkling of an eye' and Waters had never intended to murder her.

In his summing up, Justice Rowlatt stated that the question facing the jury was whether the accused had meant to kill Lily France and pointed out that Waters had said that he meant to injure her. The judge then advised them that if they believed he had meant to injure her and had killed her that was unquestionably manslaughter. Having retired for a period of about fifty minutes, the jury returned with a verdict of 'man-slaughter.'

In sentencing Waters to penal servitude for life, Justice Rowlatt added:

You have been convicted of manslaughter under the most dreadful circum-stances, because without a shadow of justification, under circumstances I am perfectly certain we have not heard of, you took the life of a young girl who went out trusting in your company. If there was ever a manslaughter only separated from a murder – a cruel murder – by a hair's breadth, this is the case.

BIBLIOGRAPHY

Books

Church, R., *More Murder in East Anglia* (Robert Hale Ltd, 1990)

Deeks, R., *Some Suffolk Murders* (Glemsford (printed by R & K Tyrrell), 1985)

Jacobs, L.C., *Constables of Suffolk: A Brief History of Policing in the County* (Suffolk Constabulary, 1992)

Mower, M., *Foul Deeds and Suspicious Deaths in Suffolk* (Wharncliffe Books, 2008)

Mower, M., *Suffolk Tales of Mystery & Murder* (Countryside Books, 2006)

Rose, A., *Lethal Witness* (Sutton Publishing Ltd, 2007)

Storey, N.R., *A Grim Almanac of Suffolk* (Sutton Publishing Ltd, 2004)

West, H.M., *East Anglia Tales of Mystery & Murder* (Countryside Books, 2003)

Wright, P., *Death Recorded: Capital Punishment in Suffolk* (Pawprint Publishing, 2006)

Newspapers and Journals

Bradford Observer

Bury & Norwich Post

Daily News

East Anglian Daily Times

Eastern Daily Press

Freeman's Journal and Daily Commercial Advertiser

Ipswich Express

Ipswich Journal

Lloyd's Weekly

Leicester Chronicle

Lowestoft Journal

Morning Post

Suffolk Standard

The *Star*

The *Times*

West Suffolk Gazette

INDEX

Other titles published by The History Press

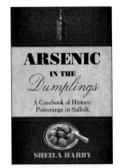

Arsenic in the Dumplings: A Casebook of Historic Poisonings in Suffolk
SHEILA HARDY

During the eighteenth and early nineteenth centuries arsenic was readily available. Of all forms of murder, poisoning is the one that is premeditated. Yet it is also the least certain way to ensure the death of the desired victim. As we learn from these cases from Suffolk's history, unintended people sometimes suffered at the hands of the poisoner. Neither has it always been possible to prove the guilt of the one who had administered the poison. This chilling collection is sure to appeal to all those interested in the shady side of Suffolk's history.

978 0 7524 5132 9

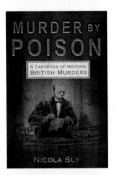

Murder by Poison: A Casebook of Historic British Murders
NICOLA SLY

Readily obtainable and almost undetectable prior to advances in forensic science during the twentieth century, poison was considered the ideal method of murder and many of its exponents failed to stop at just one victim. Along with the most notorious cases of murder by poison in the country – such as those of Mary Ann Cotton and Dr Thomas Neil Cream – this book also features many of the cases that did not make national headlines, examining not only the methods and motives but also the real stories of the perpetrators and their victims.

978 0 7524 5065 0

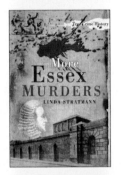

More Essex Murders
LINDA STRATMANN

This chilling follow-up to *Essex Murders* brings together more true cases, dating between 1823 and 1960, that shocked not only the county but also made headline news across the nation. They include the bloody killing of a police sergeant, a murder carried out in the depths of Epping Forest, the Dutch au pair found dead in a ditch, and a case that made criminal history in which the accused said he had strangled the victim while he was asleep.

978 0 7524 5850 2

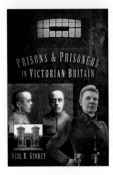

Prisons & Prisoners in Victorian Britain
NEIL R. STOREY

Featuring stories of crime and misdeeds, this fascinating book includes chapters on a typical day inside a Victorian prison, including food, divine service, exercise and medical provision; the punishments inflicted on convicts — such as hard labour, flogging, the treadwheel and shot drill; and an overview of the ultimate penalty paid by prisoners — execution. Richly illustrated with a series of photographs, engravings, documents and letters, this volume is sure to appeal to all those interested in crime and social history in Victorian Britain.

978 0 7524 5269 2

Visit our website and discover thousands of other History Press books.
www.thehistorypress.co.uk